A Daily Study in Loyalty ~~for~~
Ash Wednesday to Holy Thursday

LEAD US NOT

into

TEMPTATION

Martin Shannon, CJ

PARACLETE PRESS
BREWSTER, MASSACHUSETTS

2020 First Printing

Lead Us Not into Temptation: A Daily Study in Loyalty for Ash Wednesday to Holy Thursday

Copyright © 2020 by Martin Shannon, CJ

ISBN 978-1-64060-460-5

LIBRARY OF CONGRESS CATALOGING-IN-PUBLICATION DATA
Names: Shannon, Martin, author.
Title: Lead us not into temptation : a daily study in loyalty for Ash
   Wednesday to Holy Thursday / Martin Shannon, CJ.
Description: Brewster, Massachusetts : Paraclete Press, 2020. | Summary: "A
   daily devotional/study for Lent on the subject and the experience of
   temptation. Daily reflections on the hard school of temptation, based on
   Scriptures, inspired by the Lenten experience of a Benedictine monastic
   community. Each day's reflection includes a quotation taken from two
   works by Dietrich Bonhoeffer"-- Provided by publisher.
Identifiers: LCCN 2019035989 (print) | LCCN 2019035990 (ebook) | ISBN
   9781640604605 (trade paperback) | ISBN 9781640604612 (epub) | ISBN
   9781640604629 (mobi) | ISBN 9781640604636 (pdf)
Subjects: LCSH: Lent—Prayers and devotions. | Temptation in the Bible. |
   Bonhoeffer, Dietrich, 1906-1945--Quotations. | Benedictine movement
   (Anglican Communion)—Prayers and devotions.
Classification: LCC BX2170.L4 S465 2020 (print) | LCC BX2170.L4 (ebook) |
   DDC 242/.34—dc23
LC record available at https://lccn.loc.gov/2019035989
LC ebook record available at https://lccn.loc.gov/2019035990

10 9 8 7 6 5 4 3 2 1

Published by Paraclete Press
Brewster, Massachusetts
www.paracletepress.com
Printed in the United States of America

Contents

Preface

THE WEEK BEFORE ASH WEDNESDAY OF 2019, a small number of us from my community made a weeklong retreat to prepare for Lent and Easter. Not all of the conversations were about spiritual and liturgical things, of course, but those that spun around these topics were always lively and imaginative and, for me, sometimes taxing. As much as I enjoy collaboration, I also can find the experience challenging and sometimes even threatening. If nothing else, however, moving through those experiences together is one of the things that community is all about, though I confess that on more than one occasion I succumbed to the temptation to indulge in the solitude of my room a little longer than necessary.

During one of those conversations I raised the idea of writing a daily devotional for our community on the subject of temptation. At the time, had I known what it would require over the next six weeks, I am sure that I would not even have whispered the thought out loud. (The first step was to write the introduction "in the company" of my fellow retreatants. Remember what I just said about my ambivalent relationship with collaboration?) So, this volume is dedicated to these hearty "collaborators" who stood with me from start to finish . . . and who are still doing so. They know who they are. I can only hope they also know how grateful I am.

Introduction

*L*EAD US NOT INTO TEMPTATION IS A DAILY DEVOTIONAL/ study for Lent on the subject—we should say, the *experience*—of temptation.

Jesus taught us to pray, "Lead us not into temptation," which mysteriously implies that God *could*, and perhaps sometimes *does*. At the very least he allows it. Mark writes that the Spirit actually "drove" Jesus into the wilderness, where he was tempted by the devil (1:12). Would God really do that to me? Would he set up or allow circumstances that would put me in harm's way? In *sin's* way? I pray not, but, if I am Christ's follower, should I not expect to walk with him into the wilderness, and to face temptation in my own life? Put the other way around, should I not expect to walk in wildernesses of my own, where Christ will walk with me? In other words, isn't temptation simply a part, perhaps even a *necessary* part, of my life with Christ?

One translation of James 1:12 (RSV) reads, "Blessed is the man who endures *trial*." Another (NRSV) reads, "Blessed is anyone who endures *temptation*." In the New Testament, the same word is used for "temptation" and for "trial." That makes sense. Temptations are most certainly trials. They are difficult, painful, and sometimes even destructive. Likewise, trials, which by their very meaning cause us difficulty and pain, often tempt us to make harmful choices or follow our worst inclinations. "Have we trials and temptations?" asks the old gospel hymn. Most certainly, yes! And if we have one, we have the other.

The truth is, there is no escaping temptation. Since temptation is made up of the inevitably disastrous mix of our own desires and Satan's lies, wherever we are, wherever the devil is, there will be temptation. One of the Desert Mothers, Amma Theodora, illustrates the lesson with this story:

> There was once a monk who because of a host of temptations that afflicted him said, "I will go from this place." And when he was putting on his sandals, he saw another person also putting on his sandals, who said to him, "It is not because of me that you are leaving, is it? See, I will accompany you wherever you go."[1]

We know that, in their hour of trial, some have risen to the occasion and met the challenge valiantly. Joseph resisted the enticements of Potiphar's wife (Gen. 39:7–9); Elisha refused to be rewarded for a miracle that was wholly God's doing (2 Kgs. 5:15–16); Esther resisted concealing her true identity in order to protect her people (Esther 4:15–16); and Ananias, though he could have run the other way, did the fearful thing God asked of him when he went to see Paul (Acts 9:13–17). But I am not Joseph, nor Elisha, nor Esther, nor Ananias. I am Adam . . . and I am Eve. I fall. Regularly. So I pray as Jesus taught me. I pray that God will not lead me into temptation, because I know that, left to myself, I will always fall. I haven't the inherent strength to endure it.

---

1   Quoted in Stelios Ramfos, *Like a Pelican in the Wilderness* (Brookline, MA: Holy Cross Orthodox Press, 2000), 111.

So what's the point? If temptation is so dangerous, and so seldom overcome, what good can it possibly do? What purpose can it have? We find a clue in those profound words of Joseph to his brothers. Recalling the hatred they once had for him and the harm they brought upon him, Joseph said, "Even though you intended to do harm to me, God intended it for good" (Gen. 50:20). The same can be said about temptation: Satan (who is the tempter par excellence) means it for evil, but God means it for good. How so?

Augustine was one of a number of the church's teachers who said that it is only by temptation that he really came to know himself and came to know his God. Temptation reveals the otherwise hidden fissures in my soul, my divided heart, my conflicted thoughts, my ulterior motives. It teaches me what I am made of and what I am capable of. It purges me of my delusions about myself. François Fénelon said that temptation is like a file that scrapes off all of the rust of our self-confidence. That's how I get to know my true self. But I also get to know God. If I succeed in standing against temptation, I come to know God's power—the *only* means by which sin is resisted—and, if I fall to it, I come to know God's mercy—the *only* means by which sin is forgiven. Without the lessons taught by temptation, my spiritual life is left tepid and superficial. As Martin Luther once said, "My temptations have been my master's in divinity."

This brings us to the title, and the subject, of this devotional. From God's point of view, the purpose of temptation is to *teach* us. But, from the devil's point of view, the purpose of temptation is to *turn* us. Satan's primary aim is not to get us to do "bad things." That goal is far too short sighted (and too easy to accomplish). Satan's purpose in tempting us is to get us to switch sides, to change our allegiances, to betray our loyalty. That is the devil's long-range scheme. He wants us either to give in to temptation—in which case we flounder in guilt and shame—or to grow tired of standing against it—in which case we eventually give up. Either way, the end result he intends is the same: to separate us from God.

To understand the hard school of temptation better—and thereby to understand both ourselves and God better—perhaps when we realize that once again we have succumbed to sin's allures, rather than berating ourselves for "doing it again" (whatever *it* is), we could acknowledge the deeper harm we have done—both to ourselves and often to others—by our disloyalty to God. Then, rather than wallowing in self-disappointment, we could be awakened, even energized, with the self-realization (Jesus's parable says that the prodigal son "came to himself"): "Look what I have done. I fell for it again. I jumped the fence and ran off. That's it! I'm getting back home as fast as I can!" This is what conviction and repentance mean, and they can be the direct result of temptation—temptation resisted *and* temptation succumbed to. Recalling the words of Julian of Norwich, we can take heart: "First there is the fall; then there is the recovery from the fall. Both are the mercy of God."

Given the connection between temptation and the troubling question of our divided "loyalties," there is another aspect of temptation that must be considered as well, and Lent is a perfect time for us to do it. In my community, before we hear the call to all the other "practices" of Lent—prayer, fasting, works of love, reading and meditating on God's Word—this charge is set before us as we gather in the church on Ash Wednesday: "I invite you, therefore, in the name of the church, to the observance of a holy Lent, by *self-examination* and *repentance*." Lent is not only a time to prepare for coming temptations. It is also a time to discover, and repent for, temptations already past, temptations to which we have already given in, perhaps without our even knowing it, and, what is worse, not caring about it. Isn't that the most devious of temptations: for the devil (in cahoots with our own desires) to trip us up without our knowing it? To let us think that everything is as it should be when it is anything but? To have us believe the illusion that the desert places in our hearts are lush gardens and that dry river beds are rushing waters? If it's true that temptation raises the deeper issues of our loyalties and not just our behaviors, then perhaps the greatest trick of the devil is to get us to not pay attention.

Self-examination—presenting our lives before the enlightening work of the Holy Spirit—is the kind of "paying attention" that makes us available to God's gift of conviction and repentance. It is the only thing that can put our "fall" into the clear light of day and make "recovery from the fall" possible. It requires staying in place long enough (maybe for forty days?) to listen to the questions: Somewhere along the way, have I already "fallen" to temptation? Where do I not even know I've fallen? Have I compromised myself, grown tired of the fight, or even given up in some way? What is the besetting sin of my life that continues to give the devil an easy target? Have I forgotten what God has told me? Have I forgotten God?

Lead Us Not into Temptation

Through the days of Lent, from Ash Wednesday to Holy Thursday, with these questions (and surely more) in mind, we will look at temptation as it is described in the Bible. As we begin, let us make this our prayer:

Almighty God, whose blessed Son
was led by the Spirit to be tempted by Satan:
Come quickly to help us who are assaulted by many temptations;
and, as you know the weaknesses of each of us,
let each one find you mighty to save.
Amen.

COLLECT FOR THE FIRST SUNDAY OF LENT
BOOK OF COMMON PRAYER

■ ■ ■

A word about the quotations at the end of each day's reflection. They are taken from two works of the German pastor and theologian Dietrich Bonhoeffer (1906–1945): a series of lectures given on the creation and fall of Adam and Eve, and a six-day Bible study on the theme of temptation, given by Bonhoeffer during a retreat with former students of his underground seminary in Nazi Germany. These have been collected into a single volume.[2] In 1943, Bonhoeffer was imprisoned and, two years later, hung for his part in an anti-Nazi conspiracy to assassinate Adolf Hitler. Anyone familiar with Bonhoeffer's story knows that we are hearing from a man who knew well the dark side of human nature and who did his level best to resist it both in himself and in others.

---

2 Dietrich Bonhoeffer, *"Creation and Fall" and "Temptation,"* trans. John C. Fletcher and Kathleen Downham (New York: Simon & Schuster / Touchstone, 1997). See permissions at the back of the book for a summary of the quotations and where they may be found in the Simon & Schuster volume.

FOUR THINGS TO KNOW FIRST

God Is Faithful
1 Corinthians 10:13

"TEMPTATIONS TO SIN ARE SURE TO COME," SAID JESUS (Lk. 17:1 RSV). The Son of God himself tells us that temptation is inevitable, inescapable. Paul puts it another way when he writes to the Corinthians. He tells us that temptation is the most common of Christian experiences. Should we ever be surprised, therefore, when it comes our way?

But, just as inevitable, just as certain, is the promise of God's assistance. "The Lord knows how to rescue the godly from trial" (2 Pet. 2:9). This is the first thing we must know about temptation—*God is faithful* and never leaves us alone to face it. We cannot examine the nature of temptation (much less experience it) without first stating this truth. We may question it at times. We may lose our grip on its reality in the midst of our pain. We may even rail against a God who seems to have left us entirely on our own. But if we are going to learn anything about temptation, if we are going to see it for what it really is, we need a larger perspective. And for that, we cannot begin with a microscope. We must stop for a moment, pull back, and take in the whole picture, from heaven's point of view rather than our own.

We begin by considering temptation as it sits within the panoramic landscape of God's faithful care. It is neither the only thing in the picture, nor is it the largest. Yes, it is unmistakably present. You can't miss the black smudge it leaves in an otherwise pastoral scene. But it is surrounded by and contained within a vibrant palette of color and movement. There, in the eyes of the Artist, even the black smudge of temptation has its place. God is faithful . . . always.

> *The temptation of the devil drives the Christian afresh*
> *into the arms of Jesus Christ, the Crucified.*

The Enemy Within
James 1:12–15

THE FIRST THING WE MUST KNOW ABOUT OUR EXPERIENCE
of temptation is that *God is faithful.* The second thing we
must know is that *we are not.* As a matter of fact, we are quite
the opposite. Consider the way Genesis describes the condition
of things before the great Flood. Chapter 6 says that God saw
the wicked (not a word we use much anymore) condition of
man, and that "*every* imagination of the thoughts of his heart
was *only* evil *continually*" (v. 5 RSV). Every, only, continually—
that's a lot of superlatives! Is it any wonder we have trouble with
temptation?

Jesus said much the same thing about the pollution that
comes out of the human heart (Mk. 7:21–22). Take a look at
the list he makes, and then see if you can still say, "The devil
made me do it." To put it another way, we have "soft spots" in
our souls. Yes, the devil is the chief tempter (more about that
tomorrow). But we are temptable, and he knows right where to
aim his darts in order to strike at the most vulnerable places.
Our fight against temptation is a fight against our own worst
selves. Preparing monks who were just entering the monastery,
Aelred, abbot of Rievaulx (d. 1167), said, "You have come to
the service of God. Stand bravely and prepare your soul for
temptation." He knew what they would be facing in themselves
as they embarked on the spiritual life.

The point is, we cannot blame anyone other than ourselves when we fall to temptation. James essentially tells us that we are our own worst enemies. If we are going to grapple with temptation, we better first know who we are contending with.

The place in which all temptation originates is my evil desires. My own longing for pleasure, and my fear of suffering, entice me to let go of the Word of God.

The Tempter
1 Thessalonians 3:5

YES, WE MUST ADMIT THAT, IN THE BATTLE OF TEMPTATION, we are often our own worst enemies. But if we are to have any hope of persevering in the fight, much less prevailing, we must also identify our principal opponent—our "ancient foe" as Martin Luther describes him:

> *For still our ancient foe doth seek to work us woe;*
> *His craft and pow'r are great, and, armed with cruel hate,*
> *On earth is not his equal.*

As we begin this study of temptation, the third thing we must know is that we are engaged in a spiritual battle against one who is the mortal enemy of all human souls. Writing to the Christians in Thessalonica, Paul calls our enemy the "tempter," the one who schemes to undermine our faith, to weaken our resolve, to demoralize us, and, by every means possible, to tear us away from God. Elsewhere the Bible calls him the devil ("slanderer," John 13:2), Satan ("adversary," Job 1:6), and Apollyon ("destroyer," Rev. 9:11).

By whatever name he is called, make no mistake, the sole aim of the "tempter" is our destruction. Peter likens him to a stealthy ravenous lion, constantly on the hunt for unwitting prey (1 Pet. 5:8). He is both devious in his methods and merciless in his conquest. As Luther affirmed in his hymn, there is no equal on earth to match his malicious strength.

19

Why should we acknowledge the tempter's power in this way? Not to make us afraid, but to make us aware. In the battle of temptation, we need to know who and what we are up against, and it is not flesh and blood (see Eph. 6:12).

Temptation is a power which is stronger than any creature. It is the invasion of Satan's power into the world of creation.

A Liar and the Father of Lies
John 8:44

WE WOULD DO WELL TO LISTEN CAREFULLY WHEN JESUS describes the ways of the devil. Our Lord has intimate knowledge of his enemy (and ours), and of his methods. When he calls Satan "a liar and the father of lies," Jesus is giving us a critical insight into the devil's weaponry of choice. Lying is his most effective technique—it has certainly worked countless numbers of times—because it is his *only* technique. Satan *is* a liar and therefore he can generate nothing but lies. Paul says that he is so proficient at it, in fact, that he, the prince of all darkness, will even disguise himself as an angel of light (2 Cor. 11:14). This is deception in the extreme—calling evil good and night day.

This also means that somewhere, in all our experiences of temptation, a lie of some kind sits at the root of our struggle. Where is it? Will I recognize it for what it is, or will it be something I actually think is true? Have I always believed it and therefore grown comfortable with it? And why that particular lie? Why does the devil think he can fool me with that one? Satan is a liar to the bone, and the maker of all lies. This is one of those lessons that we forget to our peril. But if we remember it, we may be able to identify what is happening in our own hours of temptation. We may even find truth . . . the Truth.

So these are the four things about temptation that we must know for certain as we begin Lent: God is faithful; we can be our own worst enemies; the tempter par excellence is Satan himself;

21

and the devil's methods always revolve around a lie. With these in mind, we will begin by looking at seven biblical examples of temptation.

Temptation is seduction, leading astray.
Therefore it is of the devil, for the devil is a liar.

LENT
WEEK ONE

Predator Sin
Genesis 4:6—7

THIS WEEK, WE'LL LOOK AT SEVEN BIBLICAL STORIES of temptation—examples, really, of the kinds of "beasts" we are up against in the wilderness of temptation. The first is about as primal as you can get.

It is sobering to observe that little more than twenty-five verses separate the serpent's lie—"You will *not die*" (Gen. 3:4— more about this next week)—from the first act of sin recorded in the Bible—"Cain rose up against his brother Abel, and *killed* him" (Gen. 4:8). If ever there was evidence of the devil's malicious handiwork, from first planting the poisonous seed to finally reaping the bitter fruit, it is in this story.

But, before committing the brutal *act* of sin with his hands, Cain first lost his heart to the tempting *power* of sin. The word for "sin" first appears in the Bible in Genesis 4:7, when God warns Cain that his soul is at terrible risk. With words that sound both loving and stern at the same time (isn't that often how God warns?), God describes sin as a predatory beast, hungrily lurking just outside, waiting for Cain to let down his guard and unlatch the door. The story does not make explicit why Abel's sacrifice was accepted by God and Cain's was not. That's not really the point. God's ways are inscrutable, and we are often left in the dark. What is crystal clear, however, is that the power of jealousy left unattended, unchecked—unmastered by the gifts of confession and forgiveness—consumes everything in its covetous sight. (It contributed to the death of our Lord—see Matt. 27:18; Mk. 15:10). Cain's real fall to temptation did not happen when he murdered his brother, nor when he cunningly invited him to go out into the field. Cain lost to temptation much sooner, when he cherished his own wounds more than God's words.

> *Unforgiven, cherished sin is the best gateway*
> *by which the devil can invade our hearts.*

Unbelief Makes a Mess of It
Genesis 16:1–6

WAITING MAY BE UP THERE AMONG THE MOST DIFFICULT things we are asked to do by God. Partly because, at least on the surface, waiting doesn't seem like obvious work. Not like leaving your family and making home in an entirely foreign land (Gen. 12:1); or giving your life to preaching the gospel (Acts 13:2); or entering a monastery . . . for life. Those are what we call hard work. Waiting is, well, just waiting. Like sitting at a bus stop—"killing time," we say—until the bus arrives. If you decide to stop waiting, what does it matter? "I'm tired of waiting for this bus. I think I'll just walk." What can be the harm in that?

But the work of waiting, when asked to do so by God—when required to do so by God—has behind it another kind of work, a work that can be very hard indeed for the likes of us: *believing*. God made a promise to Abraham and Sarah, a promise that he repeated many times, and that he "signed" with sacrificial blood (Gen. 12:2; 13:16; 15:5–16). Is God as good as his word? The waiting—the believing—would eventually answer that question with a resounding yes. But unfortunately, not before they gave up waiting and decided to walk. And look at the mess they made by taking things into their own hands. In her doubt, Sarah even accused God of "preventing" her from having a child (Gen 16:2)! Take care. The road of unbelief intersects with accusation at many crossroads.

Abraham and Sarah succumbed to the temptation to do in the arm of flesh what could *only* be done in the power of the Holy Spirit. This just might be one of the devil's easiest and most cunning temptations—convincing us to believe more in ourselves than in God.

> *The Christian recognizes the cunning of Satan.*
> *Suddenly, doubt has been sowed in his heart,*
> *suddenly everything is uncertain.*

The Opposite of Unbelief Is Obedience
Genesis 22:1–3

NOT ALL OF THE BIBLICAL EXAMPLES OF TEMPTATION we can look at are failures. (And, as we have already said, even the "failures" are *lessons*.) Here is a "success" story, made all the more poignant by the fact that Abraham, as we saw in yesterday's reading, once fell dramatically to the temptation to turn away from God's promise. After that, what would he do years later with God's command?

It is not a stretch to read between the lines and imagine the discordant thoughts and feelings that must have been swirling through Abraham's soul when he heard God's terrible words, "Take your son, your only son Isaac, whom you love, and go to the land of Moriah, and offer him there as a burnt offering on one of the mountains that I shall show you" (Gen. 22:2 NRSV). We read this story at every Easter Vigil, and we've all learned how it spiritually foreshadows Christ's crucifixion and resurrection. This is true, but the story only means something so profound because it contains something so painful. Let's be careful lest we sand the sharp edges off these verses and miss their awful reality. God knew perfectly well what he was asking of Abraham, and he says it with his own words: he calls Isaac Abraham's *son*, his *only* son, the son whom he *loved* (v. 2). Isaac was not only the fulfillment of God's promise. He was Abraham's own flesh and blood. And God was asking—no, commanding—that Abraham kill and burn him on some nameless mountaintop.

We know how the story turns out, so we can safely conclude that Abraham withstood his fear—the temptation *not* to do what God commanded. The writer to the Hebrews tells us that Abraham's act of obedience was actually an act of faith (Heb. 11:17–19) . . . which is true of all obedience to God, isn't it?

> *The God who causes day and night to be*
> *also gives seasons of thirst and seasons of refreshment;*
> *he gives storms and peace, times of grief and fear,*
> *and times of joy.*

Great Is Our Fickleness
Exodus 32:7–8

GOD HAD BIG PLANS FOR THE CHILDREN OF ISRAEL. From the time of Abraham—by some calculations more than seven hundred years before the exodus, when this great multitude encamped at the foot of Mount Sinai was only a promise and a hope for a distant future—we read of God's faithful work on behalf of his chosen: miracles, heavenly visitations, expansive gifts of lands and fertile fields, blessings and protections, divine interventions to preserve and increase, the making of a great nation. And always, the promise. The promise to this "fewest of all peoples," this tiny clan upon whom God had set his own heart (Deut. 7:7), was that, *always*, they would be his people and he would be their God. Always?

Only a few weeks before the events described in Exodus 32, this favored people had experienced what can only be described as the most sensational act of deliverance in human history. They were not only witnesses of it. They were active participants who, looking upon their defeated captors from the shores of the Red Sea, danced and sang with jubilation:

This is my God, and I will praise him,
my father's God, and I will exalt him. (Exod. 15:2)

But less than three months later, that is not the song they were singing as they waited in the wilderness for Moses's return from the mountain. We are certainly in no position to judge their fickle ways too harshly. "You shall have no other gods before me" is the first commandment (Exod. 20:3). No wonder. In the wilderness, we have such a propensity for making false gods, especially when we are tempted to think that the One we do have isn't working . . . or isn't there . . . or isn't enough.

God shows himself in temptation not as the gracious,
the near one, who furnishes us with all the gifts of the Spirit;
on the contrary, it is as if he forsakes us, he is quite distant from us;
we are in the wilderness.

The Wrong Place at the Wrong Time
2 Samuel 11:1–4

G ENEALOGIES USUALLY DON'T MAKE FOR SCINTILLATING
reading, but they can be remarkably informative. Though
largely and not unexpectedly patriarchal, Matthew includes
four women in his well-ordered list of Jesus's ancestors: Tamar,
Rahab, Ruth, and . . . the unnamed "wife of Uriah" (Matt. 1:6).
Of course, Matthew (and everyone else) knew that her name was
Bathsheba. He could have just named her, as he did the others.
Instead, here at the opening of the New Testament, the mother
of Solomon is identified as the woman David stole for himself
from another man. What far-reaching consequences some of
our sins can have. If one is looking for a clear example of falling
to temptation, here it is. What John calls "the lust of the flesh
and the lust of the eyes and the pride of life" (1 John 2:16 RSV)
all converged within David and provoked a tragic decision as
he walked on the rooftop late that spring afternoon. He wanted
what he saw, and he had the power to take it. And he did.

But the writer of the story sets an interesting stage. David was
home, spending a leisurely day in the sun at a time when, normally,
"kings go out to battle" (2 Sam. 11:1). It's quite possible that, had
David been where he should have been—on the battlefield with
his captains—the opportunity for his transgression would not
have presented itself. By his own volition, he may have been in
the wrong place at the wrong time. Temptation cannot be
prevented, but surely it doesn't have to be invited.

We know from the whole story (see 2 Sam. 11–12)—and from Matthew's genealogy—that God not only forgave David's sin but also wove it into the very fabric of redemption. If this extraordinary drama gives us a clear example of falling to temptation, it also gives us a technicolor vision of what God can do with repentance.

> *The lust of the flesh is nothing other than*
> *the anguish of the flesh in the face of death.*

Inch by Inch
1 Kings 11:1—2

BY NOW WE HAVE SEEN ENOUGH BIBLICAL CASE STUDIES
of temptation to know that the Bible is replete with
examples of the problem. And if we are at all honest, we have
been able to locate ourselves somewhere in each of those stories.
It would be unwise to look at these men and women and to
entertain even the slightest notion that we are not made of the
same stuff as they. "So if you think you are standing . . ." (1 Cor.
10:12). Certainly the same can be said about today's example—
Solomon—not because we know anything about being married
to dozens (actually, hundreds!) of wives (1 Kgs. 11:3), but
because we know something about being disobedient to God.
Defying God always makes life complicated, but over the long
haul it can be absolutely disastrous.

The writer of 1 Kings tells us in 11:4 that, in his old age,
Solomon "turned away his heart after other gods." It is as if
the well of faithfulness to God that fed so many of his early
years gradually ran dry and evaporated away. Slowly, almost
imperceptibly . . . but irrevocably. By his waning years, Solomon's
heart for God had shriveled. Why?

Verse 2 tells it all: through his many years, over and over
again, Solomon did the very thing that God told his people
not to do. It almost doesn't matter what the specifics are. In
Solomon's case it was marrying "foreign women" who gradually
inclined his heart to follow after other gods. The point is that

he persisted in this disobedience long enough that what once had been only a temptation gradually became something quite "normal." How terrifying. Furthermore, what God said would happen as a result *did* happen. No surprise there! As was stated already, the problem with falling to temptation is not that we do "bad things," but that we switch sides, change our allegiances, and betray our loyalties.

[Satan] plans to make the flesh rebellious towards the spirit.
Satan knows that the flesh is afraid of suffering.

What Will Be the Last Word?
Acts 9:10–17

SO ANANIAS WENT" (V. 17). THOSE THREE WORDS, perhaps the most critical words in this passage, tell us that this is the story of a successful overcoming. Fortunately for Saul (Paul), fortunately for the early church, fortunately for all of us—Ananias *went*. Earlier in the story, however, three other words tell us that this ending was not necessarily a given: "But Ananias answered" (v. 13). The connection between these two brief phrases gives us another lesson in the problem of temptation.

What if God asks me to do something that I find frightening? It doesn't even have to be the scariest thing in the world, just something that makes me afraid. My immediate, and quite irrepressible, spiritual posture before God is feet planted, hands clenched, and teeth set, while my mind rapidly constructs all of the building blocks of a reasonable explanation for why this "request" cannot be met. I don't really need the devil to tempt me not to do it. He might blow on the flames of my resistance, but my fear is the thing that will start the fire. And once the fire of fear starts to burn, it can be very tempting to sit in its paralyzing warmth and not go anywhere. It made good sense for Ananias to be afraid when God called his name, telling him to get up and directing him to go and find a man named Saul. Ananias had heard the reports about this heartless persecutor of Christians. But he wasn't sure God had heard.

"But Ananias answered." Even while afraid, he kept the conversation going. And so did God. Look how God works with him, even going so far as to give Ananias a little glimpse behind the scenes—to show him the way God sees things—before still sending him on his divine errand. "So Ananias went." His fear had words . . . just not the last one.

We have all had the dream that we desire to flee
from something horrible and cannot.
This is the ever-recurring knowledge in our subconscious
of the true situation of fallen man.

LENT
WEEK TWO

Innocence
Genesis 2:25

L AST WEEK, WE LOOKED AT VARIOUS BIBLICAL EXAMPLES
of temptation that give us insight into the nature of this
problem that is common to us all—for we all live in a broken
world, thrashing about within the limits of human flesh, and,
whether or not we acknowledge it, locked in mortal combat
with an enemy who would like nothing less than to tear us apart.
Beginning this week, we look back to the first "case study" in
temptation of all time. This is the one that sets the stage for all
that are to follow—including, most importantly, Jesus's forty
days and nights in the wilderness being tempted by the devil
(more about that later).

The writer of Genesis tells us of a time when all creation was
new, when the world was whole, human flesh was flawless, and
the devil was not yet in the picture. Man and woman—God's
supreme work of self-giving, overabundant, loving creativity—
stood in a garden surveying the handiwork of heaven on earth.
This garden was their home, and it was their meeting place with
their Creator. One can imagine broad smiles on their faces as
they took in the sights around them, as they looked upon each
other, and as they moved about in the light of God's presence.
For here, in Eden, Adam and Eve enjoyed unfettered access to
their heavenly Host. Almost as if remembering it himself, the
psalmist captures the scene when he writes,

> They feast on the abundance of your house,
> and you give them drink from the river of your delights.
> For with you is the fountain of life;
> in your light we see light. (Ps. 36:8–9)

There was no shame, no embarrassment, no guilt, and therefore no hiding. Light abounded. In their nakedness, Adam and Eve were utterly transparent, visible, available, and vulnerable to each other and to their Creator. What freedom and peace they must have enjoyed from such innocence. What gladness. It's what makes the event that follows so heartrending.

The tempter is only to be found where there is innocence . . .
where there is guilt, he has already gained power.

Temptation Comes Quietly
Genesis 3:1

THE OPENING TWO CHAPTERS OF GENESIS CONCLUDE
with a scene of indescribable beauty and peace. Then, in a
single verse, the writer introduces the first ominous sign of trouble
in Paradise. At the striking of an almost imperceptible discordant
tone in an otherwise lush chord of harmony, we become abruptly
aware that something doesn't fit. The Hebrew text calls our
attention to it. In stark contrast to the innocent nakedness (Heb.
arum) of Adam and Eve, the serpent is known for his subtle
craftiness (Heb. *arom*). If you're not careful, you might miss the
difference, and, of course, this is precisely the serpent's intention.
He presents himself as a quiet innocent himself, not really all that
different from the woman who is standing before him.

For the most part, the human psyche is naturally repulsed by
snakes. Despite a variety of historical traditions that celebrate
snakes and serpents as wise, healing, and even life-giving,
for the most part the Bible reinforces our natural aversion,
presenting them as devious, poisonous, and even lethal. In the
case of Genesis 3, the serpent is the personification of evil, the
vengeful negator of all that God stands for, presenting himself in
visible form. Virtually stealing—no, perhaps actually stealing—
the lowly body of one of God's own wild creatures, the devil
disguises himself as an innocent. He says the first one of his
lies in human history, even before he speaks a single word.
Remember, he can do none other (John 8:44).

Just as the first book of the Bible introduces the devil, the last book of the Bible describes his ultimate demise (Rev. 20:2, 10). In between is the story of his sinister intentions for the human race, beginning with Adam and Eve . . . and including you and me.

The voice of the tempter does not come out of an abyss
only recognized as "Hell." It completely conceals its origin. . . .
The denial of the origin belongs to the essence of the seducer.

The Serpent Said
Genesis 3:1

THE TEMPTER COMES. NO ANNOUNCEMENT.
No warning signal. No "Beware of Who Is Approaching"
sign. And definitely no fanfare. When it comes to temptation, it
is the nature of the devil's method *not* to call attention to itself—
in fact, *not* to present itself as temptation in the first place. A
full-on frontal assault would most likely scare us away. But not
just a bit of harmless conversation.

What if the serpent had said what he was really up to in the
garden that fateful morning?

"Good morning, Eve. Let me introduce myself. My name is
Lucifer. You don't know it yet, but you can't believe a word I say.
Still, I can already tell that you want to give me a moment of your
time. (I promise that if you do, you'll wish you hadn't . . . but
that's for a later conversation.) If you'll listen to me now, in a few
minutes I'll have you feeling quite muddled in your thinking,
unsteady in your beliefs, and definitely defiant in your choices.
So, just to be clear from the get-go—my intention above all else
is to get you to rethink this 'God is good' idea you've got going.
In fact, if you stay and talk with me long enough, I'm certain I
can convince you that you'd be better off coming with me than
staying with him."

"The serpent said." Mimicking his Creator—and former
Lord—the devil speaks into the world and into the ear and soul
of the human race. But his voice is a complete counterfeit, for

45

the word he speaks is not for the purpose of creating (Gen. 1:3) but destroying. God's word gives life. The devil's word is about to take it away. "He was a murderer from the beginning," said Jesus, a thief who comes only to "steal and kill and destroy" (John 8:44; 10:10). But none of this is apparent when he first steps (or slithers?) onto the scene. All he does is speak.

We should never argue with the devil about our sins,
but we should speak about our sins only with Jesus.

Did God Say?
Genesis 3:1

W<small>E TAKE ONE MORE DAY TO CONSIDER</small> G<small>ENESIS</small>
3:1, for with this verse, the opening act of humanity's
first experience with temptation begins: the serpent *enters*; the
serpent *speaks*; the serpent *asks a question*. By paying attention
to these incremental steps of the tempter, we can learn a good
deal about what to expect in our own times of trial. Remember
that the serpent's purpose is to bite in such a way that the victim
walks away with no more than a curious sense of uneasiness,
otherwise unaware that he or she has been wounded. So
here, under the guise of a simple, even a reasonable-sounding
question, the tempter begins to administer his venom. "Did
God say?" The question does two things.

First, by using and twisting God's own words, the question
casts doubt upon God's good intentions, suggesting that the
man and woman may not know their Creator as well as they
think they do. "Did God say, 'You shall not eat of *any* tree?'"
The serpent knows perfectly well that God did *not* say this. In
fact, quite the opposite! God said, "You may *freely eat*" (Gen.
2:16). Only one tree was off limits. Only one. All the rest were
completely available for picking. "Did God say?"—thus the toxic
seeds of confusion, doubt, and accusation are sown.

Second, and perhaps more ominously, the serpent's question
invites a response, and (as we shall see tomorrow) once she gives
her answer, Eve also begins to give her soul. It's the questions

that get to us, isn't it? Not the blatant accusation, "God is mean!" We usually see that lie coming a mile away. But the questions. They're different. They slip in like darts and strike at our soft underbellies—"Is this really the way it's supposed to be? Is God really like that? Did God say?" This is how the tempter starts a conversation . . . and aims to end with a conversion.

> *"Has God really said?"*
> *In the abyss of this question, Adam sinks,*
> *and with him the whole of mankind.*

The Woman Said
Genesis 3:2–3

THE SERPENT HAD (AND STILL HAS) A PLAN. HE KNEW
he'd be able to goad Eve into a conversation by asking a
question that she could not resist answering. He made it sound
like he didn't quite get it—"Did God say you can't eat any of this
fruit? That seems a bit severe, doesn't it?" Stupid snake. She'd set
this confused creature straight. "No, that's not what God said at
all. He said that we *could* eat of all the trees . . . well, except one.
He said not to eat that one . . . oh, and not to touch it either."

"Don't touch it either?" It could make sense, I suppose, but
there is no record at all of God saying that. Eve actually *overstated* what God had commanded. She made it sound like God's
restrictions were tighter than what he'd said, maybe even slightly
unreasonable. Is it possible that the serpent's question struck a
nerve in Eve? Like a child who is told one afternoon that she
can't go out to play, she betrays her annoyance when she tells her
friend, "I can't come out today . . . and probably not the rest of
the week either (pout)."

The serpent presented God falsely. But then, so did Eve. He
got her arguing on his terms, and so her answer is as false as his
question. Her attempt at a smart reply only revealed her own
misgivings about God. And this makes way for the serpent's
final strike. By exaggerating God's instructions, Eve gives away
a hint at what she may actually be thinking, that God is being
just a little bit hard. There seems to be an ever so small—but,

49

from the serpent's point of view, ever so profitable—accusation against God's goodness. Now, thinks the serpent, that's the gripe that I was looking for. In a minute, she and I could see eye to eye.

What ever possesses us to think that we can best the devil at his own game?

> *Let us be on our guard against such cunning exaggerations of God's command. The evil one is certainly in them.*

You Will Not Die
Genesis 3:4

BY FOOLISHLY THINKING THAT SHE COULD ARGUE WITH the deceiver, Eve played right into his hands. As we have seen, her intention to set the serpent straight about what God had really said (as if it's a good thing God has us around to explain him) only revealed her own hidden questions about God's integrity. Is he just? Is he asking too much? Is he keeping something from us? Thus the tempter recognized in Eve—and thereby in Adam since they were bone of bone and flesh of flesh—the possibility of a kindred spirit, someone like himself, whose quiet, even unrecognized grievance against her Creator could be stirred into full-fledged rebellion. Actually, convincing her to eat the forbidden fruit would be easy, only a baby step away from convincing Eve that her hunch was right. God may not be telling the whole truth.

The queen of all lies is to claim that the truth, spoken by Truth himself, is a lie—to call light darkness and darkness light (Isa. 5:20). "You will not die." A bold, blatant, outright lie that, for some strange reason, now felt true to Eve. "It's beginning to come clear to me now," she thinks. "What this serpent is saying makes more sense than what my Maker said. I had a sneaking suspicion all along."

Isn't this the sort of temptation we have all experienced? The serpent engages us in a conversation that comes right on the heels of an experience that has already raised in our souls an unexpressed question about God's word, or God's will, or God's love—usually an experience that has caused us some pain. In such a conversation, God becomes the third wheel. We stop talking *with* God and start to talk *about* God. God becomes a third party in the discussion, the object of our evaluation. It is then that the serpent bites. "You will not die." The lie has been offered . . . and we are ready to take it.

> *Thus the conversation goes on—*
> *the first conversation about God. . . .*
> *It is not prayer, or calling upon God together,*
> *but speaking about God,*
> *going beyond him.*

You Will Be Like God
Genesis 3:4

THE SERPENT, SEIZING HIS OPPORTUNITY WHEN EVE TRIES to argue with him, speaks the blatant lie—"you will not die"—with such authority and believability, we might add, that Eve remains silent at the outburst. Meeting no resistance from her, not even a feeble "Wait, that's not what our Maker said," the serpent works to plunge the lie even deeper. Having successfully planted the seed of doubt in her mind, he now poisons the soil of her heart. For he knows, once the heart is corrupted, the mind can be convinced of almost any lie imaginable.

"God said that you would die. Not true. He's just trying to scare you, to cover the *real reason* he wants to keep you from that fruit. The truth is, if you eat it, you'll know what he knows. You'll be just like him. And that's something he does not want. God is not protecting you. He's misleading you." The serpent lied about God's word. Now he lies about God's character. He calls God's own nature into question. As the father of lies himself, the tempter works to convince humanity (because he himself is convinced) that God is the real liar. In one brief sentence, he turns the created world upside down.

The serpent expects (perhaps justifiably) that the man and woman might want the same thing he wants—to be equal to God. The sad thing is, Adam and Eve are *already* like God. They have been handmade in his image, meaning that all of the qualities of his life are to be reflected in theirs—goodness, creativity, imagination, generosity, justice, love, joy. In what way could they be more like God than they already are? They could *know* more. They could determine for themselves what is good and what is evil. No need for imposed rules . . . no need for a teacher . . . no need for God. That added lie—"you will be like God"—introduced us to the possibility of pride, and once pride is embraced, a fall is inevitable.

> *Satan does not fill us with hatred of God,*
> *but with forgetfulness of God.*

LENT
WEEK THREE

The Woman Saw the Tree
Genesis 3:6

SOMETHING HAPPENS BETWEEN THE LAST WORDS WE HEAR
from the serpent—"you will be like God"—and Eve's act
of taking the fruit. To this point we can visualize her more or
less face-to-face with her tempter. She's been carrying on a vain
argument that we now realize, given her choice to engage in it in
the first place, she was doomed to lose from the very beginning.
We see her turning from the serpent to face the tree, and as
she does, the writer almost lets us hear the stirrings that this
produces in her soul. Reasonable thoughts are considered—"the
tree was good for food"; desire is awakened—"it was a delight
to the eyes"; human pride is born—"the tree was to be desired
to make one wise."

The serpent has accomplished his foul work. He can do no
more. He need do no more. The source of Eve's temptation has
moved from outside her—the serpent—to insider her—the soul.
The serpent's lie is transformed into Eve's action, but not before Eve
herself is transformed into a willing participant. The woman sees the
fruit in a new way. Only an hour or so earlier that day it represented
her Maker's authority, its very forbiddenness reminding her that
she neither created nor ruled the garden. The fruit was an object of
caution, perhaps even dread. But now, after entertaining the lies of
the serpent, it had become an object of desire.

Eve is now on her own. Having removed herself from the
protective covering of God's command, she is left alone with

her own thoughts and desires to guide her decision. They would never be enough to help her resist what she saw before her—fruit that would taste delicious . . . that looked delightful . . . that could make her like God. Why would anyone *not* eat it?

> *Adam is no longer creature. He has torn himself away from his creatureliness. [He] no longer needs the Creator, he has become a creator himself.*

She Also Gave
Genesis 3:6

TEMPTATION IS A LONELY BUSINESS. FOR WHATEVER REASON (the writer of Genesis does not explain why) Eve was left alone to face the serpent. Where was Adam? We are left to imagine various scenarios—Adam was nearby but not in earshot of the conversation; Eve left Adam's side but perhaps shouldn't have; Adam left Eve to wander alone and definitely shouldn't have. Taking the text at face value, however, we come to the same conclusion: the serpent struck when Eve was by herself. No one to support her. No one to interrupt and say, "Hold on a minute. Serpent, you stop talking—Eve, you stop listening!" No one to take Eve's hand and help her to turn her back and simply walk away. From the serpent's point of view (remember, the wolf's objective is to *scatter* the sheep, John 10:12), Eve's solitude provided the ideal opportunity to make his stealthy assault. Darkness feeds on isolation.

All that is now left for the serpent's scheme to achieve its successful end is for Eve to act. And it is precisely here, as we watch her reaching out to take the fruit, that suddenly (and belatedly) we awaken to the tempter's full plan. She *took*, she *ate* . . . and she also *gave*. Adam is now on the scene, standing with her, with open hand receiving the forbidden fruit. And he ate too. Temptation may be a lonely business, but the bitter consequences suffered by a vanquished soul spread like a cancer far beyond its isolated beginnings. Because we are speaking of a

59

spiritual battle ("we do not contending against flesh and blood," Eph. 6:12 RSV), we are also speaking of spiritual effects. The fall of one soul has implications for others. It does not matter that Eve picked the fruit for herself and that Adam took the fruit from Eve. Because neither of them remained submitted to the word of God, their transgression is the same and equally devastating. The disease is spread. All creation begins to groan.

The word "disobedience" does not exhaust the facts of this case.
It is revolt. . . . It is defection.
The Fall affects the whole of the created world
which is henceforth plundered.

Then . . .
Genesis 3:7

WHAT DID THE SERPENT PROMISE WOULD BE THE OUTCOME from eating the fruit?—"God knows that when you eat of it your eyes will be opened, and you will be like God, knowing good and evil" (Gen. 3:5). Had Adam and Eve held the fruit to their lips with a shiver of happy expectation for what was about to come next? As they bit down, did they wonder how they would feel when they became "like God"? What an awful realization must have come over them as they swallowed. It must have struck like a hammer blow to their gut. In an instant, the man and woman plummet from anticipation to regret, from lighthearted innocence to oppressive shame. What a dreadful change can come from a moment of defiance in the kingdom of God. Dreadful, and devastatingly irreversible (though never unredeemable—but that is for a later story).

Yes, their eyes *were* "opened," but not at all in the way they'd hoped. They had certainly seen themselves before, but it had been without self-consciousness, without embarrassment or shame. It hadn't mattered that they were naked, because nakedness was . . . well, it just *was*. They simply *were*. But now, their disobedience had plunged them into a world that they could not see clearly. This new "seeing" was distorted by guilt, a vision clouded by shame. All that had appeared before as simply being "right" and as it should be now appeared "wrong" and threatening. Is this what knowing good and evil felt like? Is this what it

61

meant to "be like God"? Why was it, then, that all they wanted to do was to hide themselves from each other?

They also knew, with what must have been a mortifying insight, that they had been utterly deceived by the serpent. Eve especially must have shaken her head with humiliation as she recalled the scintillating conversation that had led to her terrible decision. Each deceptive word of the tempter must have burned inside her like a red-hot poker. Those are the kinds of conversations we play over and over and over again in our heads, pathetically hoping that we can make them come out differently. But it was not to be. Guilt was now Adam and Eve's new adversary, and no amount of self-sewn fig leaves and loincloths could protect them from its crippling assault. This enemy lives inside, and once it takes up residence in the human heart it does not leave willingly.

It was their own fault that they now felt the way they did. They knew it. They could see their nakedness. They could see that they had been deceived. And though so many other things now looked shadowy and confusing, they could see one other thing as clear as day—they had betrayed their Maker. So, they must have known, too, that it would be only a matter of time before they would have to face him.

Man's shame is his reluctant acknowledgement . . . of God. [Shame] must give witness to its own fallen state.

The Dying Begins
Genesis 3:8

GOD, BEING GOD, KNEW WELL WHAT ADAM AND EVE had done. Not only what they had done, but also what they were experiencing as a result. God, more than they, knew the consequences they would suffer and, in fact, were already beginning to suffer. He knew them better than they knew themselves. Being God, he also must have known all the events that came before—the entrance of the serpent, his vile exchange with Eve, Adam's absence, and all the inner acrobatics of their souls that led to their decision to take and eat.

Yet the writer presents us with a tender image of an as-yet-unaware Lord God coming into the garden to take a walk with his beloved creatures. The Creator, who under the circumstances would have been entirely justified in bursting onto the scene with righteous indignation, instead comes quietly, even kindly. He cannot be hoping that his errant children will be there to meet him, to humbly admit to their transgression. Can he? What gentleness confronts us here. What affection. What availability. "Where are you?" God calls (Gen. 3:9). It would not be the last time he'd come in lowliness, looking for his children.

On the other hand, what are Adam and Eve doing? While God—the offended One—comes in search of his children, they—the offenders—run away to hide. Is this the meaning of tragedy? The most immediate price of their rebellion, as they stood there in shame, was the death of their direct connection with each other—"Cover up!" But the ultimate price was the death of their connection with God—"Hide!" Truthfulness was a fatality in this drama. Tragic . . . for it might have been a remedy.

"And before him no creature is hidden, but all are naked and laid bare to the eyes of the one to whom we must render an account" (Heb. 4:13).

Man has suddenly fallen from God and is still in flight.
The Fall is not enough for him; he cannot flee fast enough.

Not My Fault
Genesis 3:9–13

As gently as God enters the garden and as lovingly as he seeks out his children, to the guilty Adam and Eve he comes as an adversary. "I was afraid," said Adam. There had been no talk of fear in the garden before this day. What was Adam now afraid of? "Fear has to do with punishment," wrote the apostle John. "There is no fear in love" (1 John 4:18). Yesterday we said that truth died in Paradise. The other fatality was love.

Now that the toxin of rebellion was ingested, it coursed through the man and woman's souls poisoning every corner—thoughts, affections, desires, imaginations, dreams. All were now infected. And because of that, though they didn't know it yet, they were about to fall into another temptation. This time, however, there was no serpent to beguile them. Only their own hearts and their own words. Now who has become the craftiest of God's creatures?

With what almost sounds like respect—giving them the benefit of the doubt, or at least giving them time to come clean—God asks Adam and Eve *if* they have eaten from the forbidden tree. Their response is immediate and surprisingly spiteful. Without even a quick "yes, but," they each place the blame on someone else. The word "blame" comes from the Greek word for blaspheme, which means to speak evil of God or of sacred things. It's not a word we hear or use much anymore, which is ironic, since there has never been a shortage of it. When I blame someone else for a fault that is my own, I revile the image of God in my brother or sister. It is no different from taking the Lord's name in vain. Come to think of it, blaspheming is precisely what Adam and Eve did when they were confronted. "The woman . . . the serpent." They both (maybe not so craftily) deflected the responsibility for their sin onto another. But not just anyone. With "the Fall" came a soaring rise of human pride that knew no bounds. Their accusation (for it is patently impossible to excuse oneself without accusing another) did not stop with their "neighbor." It was the woman *God* gave and the serpent *God* created who were to blame. And God has been taking the blame . . . *our* blame . . . ever since.

> *Instead of surrendering,*
> *Adam falls back on one art learned from the serpent,*
> *that of correcting God.*

To Dust
Genesis 3:14—19

THE DEED HAS BEEN DONE. IT IS FINISHED. HUMANITY'S original act of sedition against the rule of the Creator—no, not only against the rule but against the Creator himself—has reached its bitter end. What's more, disobeying God is not enough. God must then be accused. In this, Adam and Eve present their ultimate defiance. Their act of uprising has been sealed by their act of blaming, and there is no going back.

Man and woman have sunk to their lowest depths. Their relationships with each other and with the creation from which they themselves received their being have been fractured beyond any hope of their making repairs. Community is the collateral damage of both their rebellion against God and the pride they assumed as their cover-up. They have inflicted such damage to themselves, and thereby to the world around them, that from that time forward pain will supplant peace as the prevailing force that defines their everyday lives. Ironically, Eve will suffer anguish in the very act of bringing forth new life. Her relationship with Adam will be fraught with conflicting desires for both intimacy and autonomy. Adam will be at perpetual war with the ground from which he came. What was created to be the source of his well-being will become the cause of his undoing. The very soil he tills for food will inevitably consume his body.

Both the serpent and the first couple had been deadly wrong. "For in the day that you eat of it you shall die," said God to his beloved children (Gen. 2:17). Now, the dust where the serpent is cursed to crawl is the same dust where the man and the woman are consigned to die. God had never lied to them. For the wages of sin is death.

With curse and promise God speaks to fallen, unreconciled, fleeing Adam. Adam is preserved alive in a world between curse and promise, and the last promise is the permission to die. Paradise is destroyed.

Turned
Genesis 3:22–24

WITH THE EXPULSION OF ADAM AND EVE FROM THE GARDEN
of Eden, the serpent's plan was brought to its dreadful
completion. In every way, the tempter had accomplished
what he set out to do. His fiendish work of temptation had
succeeded. God "drove out the man" from the only home he had
ever known, from the place of his beginning, the place of his
belonging. Adam, who had been shaped from the fertile ground
of the garden, and in every way belonged to that ground, was
yanked up by his roots and cast away into an arid wasteland that
he would eventually have to call his home. Once he and his wife
stood outside the guarded gate looking in, they would always
be strangers to Paradise (Eph. 2:12), left with only memories
of what might have been. In that moment, the serpent . . . won.

How is this so? Remember the following lines from the
introduction to these Lenten reflections: "From the devil's point
of view, the purpose of temptation is to *turn* us. Satan's primary
aim is not to get us to do 'bad things' . . . Satan's purpose in
tempting us is to get us to switch sides, to change our allegiances,
to betray our loyalty. That is the devil's long-range scheme."

When Adam and Eve made their fatal choice to disobey
God, they turned—away from God and toward a new sovereign.
Their expulsion from Eden, therefore, is not the creation of but
rather the recognition of their new citizenship. By their act of
treachery they forfeited their status in the garden. They *sided*

with God's enemy, and in doing so they became *subject* to him. From this new allegiance, everything that belonged to the old one would now be brought into question. From that point on, the man and woman would mimic the words and ways of their foul master. God and his ways would always be questioned, doubted, scrutinized . . . and ultimately rejected.

From the time of Adam's expulsion from paradise, every man is born with this question, which Satan has put in Adam's heart. That is the first question of all flesh: "Has God really said?"

LENT
WEEK FOUR

For Us and for Our Salvation
Matthew 3:17

Through the second and third weeks of Lent, we have been examining the account of Adam and Eve's temptation by the serpent in the garden of Paradise. Actually, that may not be the right way to put it. Perhaps it's more accurate to say that we have been *examined by* the story—weighed in the severe accuracy of its balances . . . and, like Belshazzar the Chaldean king, we are "found wanting" (Dan. 5:27). Genesis 3 is less history than it is autobiography, and sad pieces of our life's story can be read in every verse.

There is also a second great story of temptation in the Bible. We'd like this one to be autobiographical, but it's not. Not yet anyway. If we learn from the first story—which mostly means bearing our responsibility for repeating it, again and again and again—then the second story offers us some genuine and lasting hope. In fact, it's only *because* of the second story, a story that we really had nothing to do with (except making it necessary!), that we have hope of finding a different ending for the first. In the coming days of Lent, we turn our attention from Adam and Eve in the garden to Jesus in the wilderness.

The silent years of Jesus's life come to a very public conclusion on the banks of the Jordan River. Humbly submitting himself to the laws of God, and thereby confirming his obedience to the Father, Jesus bows his head and surrenders his body to the baptism of John. Then, as he rises from the water, the Father introduces him to the world: "This is my Son, the Beloved." Do you remember Adam and Eve, just before the appearance of the serpent, standing together in the Garden of Eden, innocent, naked, and unashamed (Gen. 2:25)? The new Adam (1 Cor. 15:45–47) now stands before us. And though he is the Son of God—*because* he is the Son of God—what he is about to suffer will be entirely for our sake.

> *The temptation which led to man's fall and the temptation which led to Satan's fall—all other temptations in human history have to do with these two stories of temptation. Either we are tempted in Adam or we are tempted in Christ.*

Led into Temptation
Matthew 4:1

IN THE WORDS OF THE LORD'S PRAYER, WE REGULARLY ASK
that the Father will "lead us not into temptation." But, for
God's own Son, "into temptation" was precisely where he was
led. It is where he *had* to be led. Both Matthew and Luke tell us
this (see Lk. 4:1). Mark is even more emphatic. He writes that
immediately after Jesus was baptized, he was *driven* by the Spirit
into the wilderness (Mk. 1:12). Jesus would spend three years
delivering the good news, by every means imaginable, but not
before first facing the hateful power of the evil one. What Adam
and Eve failed to do in the garden, Jesus, the Son of Man, would
do in the desert.

"Into the wilderness"—seen directly against the tragic back-
drop of Adam and Eve's expulsion from the Garden of Eden, the
Judean desert is our place of banishment. It is the barren land
outside the gate where the cursed ground brings forth thorns
and thistles (Gen. 3:18), and where the serpent strikes at the
heel of his victims (Gen. 3:15). It is a familiar landscape to our
souls, for since the time of our parents' betrayal, it has been our
homeland. Here, so very, very far from Paradise, God's Son will
subject himself to the vicious assaults of the ruler of that land.

And for this the point cannot be overstated—Jesus was
tempted *as one like us* (Heb. 2:17). If we do not believe the
enormity of this truth, that God in human flesh endured perilous
conflict with his enemy (and ours), then there is no hope of our

deliverance from the dominion of darkness (Col. 1:13). Jesus's perseverance through temptation means nothing to mortal men and women if he did not experience it as a genuine threat, not only to his mission, but to his very existence. What a profound mystery. After Adam and Eve failed to resist the serpent's enticement and ate of the forbidden fruit, the Lord God said, "Behold, the man has become like one of us" (Gen. 3:22 RSV). Now, as we find in the wilderness a lonely figure standing eye to eye with the face of hell, we whisper in awe, "Behold, God has become like one of us."

"Lead us not into temptation."
He who taught the disciples to pray in this way was Jesus Christ, who alone must have known what temptation was.

The Tempter Came and Said
Matthew 4:3

NO FORM OF A SERPENT THIS TIME. NO DISGUISE.
With no need to hide his true identity, the devil comes
face-to-face with Jesus as "the one-who-is-tempting" (Gk.)—
the one who places obstacles, hinders progress, sows confusion,
negates good, distorts truth, perverts beauty, darkens the mind,
accuses the heart, turns the soul. The only Son of God was well
acquainted with his enemy. Certainly the eternal Son must
have watched as the "son of the Dawn" was thrown down from
heaven, banished from serving in the divine courts to reign in
the "depths of the Pit" (see Isa. 14:12–15; Rev. 12:7–9). The Son
must have watched then, and known that the day in time would
come when he too would leave the hosts of heaven—under
his own volition and moved wholly by love—to descend to do
mortal combat with this ancient foe. Alone, in some forsaken
corner of the Judean desert, that day had come.

As Jesus prayed and fasted, walked and slept, had the
tempter been lying in wait all the time, lurking behind rocks
and hiding in the scrub? Slyly and patiently leering as Jesus
grew weaker and weaker, holding his tongue until just the right
time to strike? Matthew tells us that, after forty days, Jesus was
"famished." It must have been the lowest ebb of human strength.
Make no mistake. We are a mysterious union of body, soul, and
spirit (see 1 Thess. 5:23), so much so that what happens to one
part of this intimate trinity deeply affects the others. Just as

sorrow of heart can bring on illness in body, so can bodily pain sap strength from the soul and dull the spirit. This was Jesus's moment of vulnerability. This was when "the tempter came and *said to him.*" There'd been another fateful day when this snake of a thing had spoken. Long ago. In a lush garden and not this God-forsaken wilderness. He'd been the first to speak then too. And he'd prevailed. No doubt, he was expecting to do it again.

If Jesus was to help man, who is flesh,
he had to take upon himself
the whole temptation experience of the flesh.
Even Jesus Christ was born [in the flesh] with the question:
"Has God really said?"—yet without sin.

If You Are the Son of God
Matthew 4:3

T HE GOADING CHALLENGE THE DEVIL PUTS BEFORE JESUS
is not a demand to be convinced that he is the Son of
God. The devil knows perfectly well who Jesus is. Even his evil
underlings know who they are dealing with when they see Jesus
of Nazareth (see Mk. 1:24). No, this is not a call for proof. It is
a sneering cry of mockery, the devil's strike at what Jesus holds
dearest above all else—his identity as the only Son of his Father.
Jesus is at the threshold of his ministry, and already he hears the
scornful words that will be shouted out in the closing minutes of
his life—"*If you are the Son of God*, come down from the cross"
(see Matt. 27:39–44).

Both in the desert and at the cross, this is a particularly
contemptuous address that could be made to no one else but
Jesus. It is a handmade temptation, diabolically designed for
the Son of God. "If you are the Son of God, then what are you
doing suffering out here in the middle of nowhere? You can
do something about that. You're God's Son. You think you're
so important. Let's see." It is the devil's attempt to get Jesus to
engage with him at *his* level, on *his* terms. Remember how he
addressed Eve by dangling out that enticing question—"Did
God say?"

Whatever his opening ploy may be, the tempter will always
lead with something "attractive," something to capture our
attention or make us turn to "look" at him, even if it is in anger.

Furthermore, just by addressing Jesus in this way, the devil is tempting him to misuse the very thing that is dearest to him, to pervert his identity, and to squander it by some act of proud indignation and self-defense. "I'll show you!" says the child who is mocked in the playground or slighted by a friend. "I'll show you!" imagines the adult who thinks he isn't taken seriously or wonders if she's being ignored. If the tempter can get a rise out of Jesus, to make him defend himself and preserve his reputation, all the better. He will win with the first blow.

> *Jesus is tempted in his flesh, in his faith,*
> *and in his allegiance to God.*
> *All three are the one temptation—*
> *to separate Jesus from the Word of God.*

Change These Stones
Matthew 4:3

BEFORE YOU READ TODAY'S REFLECTION, TRY THIS EXPERIMENT. You are given a magic wand (really, it works!) and you are told that, immediately, without any time to think (. . . or pray!), with a single flick you can change *anything* you want to change. What is it that you want to change? Time's up. Decide. Now!

What did you change? Did you bring peace to the Middle East? Did you cure cancer? Did you eradicate all famine or disease? Okay, maybe it was something closer to home. Did you feed the poor, clothe the naked, free the captives? All right, closer? Did you contribute to a charity, build someone a home, give an anonymous gift? No, still not close in enough? How about one of these: did you pay off your debts, resolve your family conflicts, find something you lost, get that one thing for yourself that has always been out of reach?

If you chose anything from the first lists, or anything like them, then you don't really need to read further. Not today anyway. For the moment, you are living selflessly and generously. That's good. But if (like this writer) your choice was closer to the last list, then reading on may be of interest.

■   ■   ■

The seducer came to Jesus knowing full well that the Son of God had the *power* to change stones into bread. The eternal Word, by whom the entire universe was spoken into being out of *nothing*, could certainly tell a few stones to become loaves of bread. Child's play. Jesus *could* do it, but *would* he? The tempter would play his first card to find out, because he knew that, in addition to having power, at that moment Jesus also had something else. He had *pain*. He was hungry, thirsty, exhausted, weak, and alone. Jesus's need for food was legitimate and, out in the middle of this wasteland, there was only one way to get it. He could create it. He could use his divinity to satisfy his humanity.

What happens when we are in need or in pain? As our pain grows bigger, doesn't our world grow smaller? Sometimes all we have room for is our own distress. So we want things to change. We *need* them to change. We want desperately for things to be other than what they are . . . we want stones not to be stones anymore. We want them to be bread. What if we had the power to make it so?

This is what the devil was after—to set Jesus at odds within himself, to set his humanity *against* his divinity and to fan the flames of discord between them. Ultimately, his aim was to separate the Son from his Father. Ever since the Fall of Adam and Eve, the things of the spirit and the things of the flesh— the ways of the Creator and the ways of the created—have been in conflict (Gal. 5:17). By the mystery of the incarnation, Jesus bears this conflict in his own person. The Son of God who is also the Son of Man brings flesh and spirit together and keeps them united. He did not come to destroy the flesh, but to redeem it, to bring it back into the effortless, free, and joyful service of God. If Jesus allows his flesh and its cries to have the final word, to be the predominant voice of his will, then he dooms us to the same fate. He can never save us from "this body of death" (Rom. 7:21–24).

No one will argue the point that Jesus is in genuine need of food and water. The temptation before him, however, was not to eat, but to cast love aside and to use his divine power for self-serving purposes. Would the Father's will and the Father's love be enough to sustain his Son? Or would Jesus forgo his Father's will and forget his Father's love in favor of satisfying himself?

Would he be a magician . . . or a Savior?

(So, back to the opening experiment—did the thought occur to you to just put the wand down . . . and do nothing? It didn't to me.)

Satan tempts Jesus in the weakness of human flesh. . . .
He wishes to set his Godhead against his manhood.

A Blow from the Side
Matthew 4:5–6

IT IS PROBABLY SAFE TO SAY THAT TEMPTATIONS RARELY come one at a time in a neat, predictable, and manageable order. Testings of the human soul, especially those imposed by the *enemy* of our souls, are not like multiple-choice questions set out in a list so that, when you have finished one, you can take your time until you're ready to answer the next. They are more like diving to the ground to dodge an oncoming (and very hard-packed) snowball, only to stand back up and entirely miss seeing the (even harder-packed) one coming at us from the side. Whether or not you fall to the first one, or successfully knock it down, you can be sure that another one may already be on the way; and, if you need time to "get ready" for it, then you are already too late to see it coming.

The devil dramatically raised the ante after Jesus resisted the first assault. (Next week, we'll look at *how* Jesus handled each attack; for now we are concentrating on the temptations themselves.) First, in an instant of time, the seducer transports Jesus from the barren wilderness to the peak of the temple in Jerusalem. We should not underestimate the disorienting effect of such a sudden and drastic change in the setting. Remember, this was a real physical assault, every bit as much as it was a spiritual one. Scary or even just unfamiliar landscapes in our lives can become fertile ground for the sower of lies to plant his toxic seeds. The tempter will use whatever means possible to "soften his target."

85

Second, and after once again striking at Jesus's relationship to the Father with his opening, "If you are the Son of God," the accuser adds another devilish form of that age-old question, "Did God say?" What brazen deceitfulness! By quoting the written Word of God he aims to subvert the incarnate Word of God. With such slickness the father of lies takes something that is true, something that is good, something meant to encourage and to strengthen, and he twists it into the means of hurt and ruin. What do you do if you just don't see it coming?

> *[Satan] piles on his temptation*
> *by himself quoting God's Word against Jesus.*
> *Even Satan can use God's Word in the struggle.*

The Devil Showed Him
Matthew 4:8

FOR THE DEVIL'S THIRD AND FINAL (FOR THE TIME BEING) temptation of Jesus, the pinnacle of the temple was not a high-enough elevation. The seducer was now preparing to launch a full and unconcealed head-on attack. This would be his coup d'état. No camouflaged approach; no opening challenge to Jesus's identity as the Son of God; no devious quoting of Scripture. This would be temptation "in the raw," and for such unveiled aggression, only the loftiest and most dizzying height would do. He needs the advantage of the high ground. So, like an unholy vagrant trespassing on holy ground (how many mountaintops did *God* use to speak to his people?), the devil takes over the peak of one of God's own creations. He dares to make a sacred site—as he will a sacred time, or a sacred *life*—into the launching ground for his devilish works. (By the way, look at how much quick moving around the tempter is doing in this story. Could this give us a clue to the meaning of stability—to stand secure, patient, unyielding, and *grounded*, in the midst of the swirling "chaos" of the devil's frenzied activities?)

We have come to expect subtlety in the devil's methods, but where is it here? There isn't any. The tempter is unmasked for what he truly is as he shows Jesus "all the kingdoms of the world *and their splendor*," for by doing so he reveals his own primal lusts and desires. He supposes that, being man, the Son of Man would naturally want what he, the son of perdition, wants—that is, the kingdom, the power, and the glory, forever and ever! He must have thought that *showing* Jesus the world's glory would be akin to presenting the forbidden tree to Eve, who found its fruit to be "a delight to the eyes" (Gen. 3:6).

Jesus could have ended his battle with the devil after the second temptation, or even after the first. But we must remember that, as God in human flesh, Jesus had to be tempted *in every way* as we are. This certainly is one of them. Using the sacred ground of human senses as his stage, the devil presents his tempting visions, sometimes in flagrantly raw forms. But in doing so, he is always aiming through the eyes and straight for the heart, the true home of human desire and want. To withstand such fiery darts, mustn't we begin by filling our vision with something stronger, something purer, something truer?

> *There is only one stronger reality to be set against*
> *the exclusive reality of desire and of Satan:*
> *the image and the presence of the Crucified.*

LENT
WEEK FIVE

I Will Give to You
Matthew 4:9

FROM THE MOUNTAINTOP, THE EVIL ONE LOOKS DOWN
upon all the empires of the world and shows them to the
Son of Man as if they were so many trinkets in the palm of his
hand. There is such irony in the scene, for he who has raised
himself to such lofty heights is the same one whom God has cast
down to Sheol and to the depths of the Pit (Isa. 14:15). Never-
theless, he is the "ruler of this world" (John 12:31), the "prince of
the power of the air" (Eph. 2:2). High places—in all their varied
forms—are his playgrounds.

"All these I will *give you*," the tempter boastfully says to Jesus,
as if he were at one and the same time the richest and the most
generous being on the planet. "Look what I can offer you—it is
all *mine*, and I will *give* all of it to you." As "in your face" as the
devil's third temptation is—the temptation of power—there is
also a venomous and conniving side to it. Read Philippians 2:5–
11, the evocative hymn of Jesus's death and resurrection that
the church has made the central theme of Holy Week (*Christus
factus est*). The most important word may be the first word of
verse 9—"therefore." Jesus was exalted by the Father (he did not
exalt himself) *because* he first emptied himself in the way of
the cross. Jesus Christ is Lord because Jesus Christ is Lamb. No
death, no resurrection.

Wrapped inside the temptation to power (for temptations
often have many layers), what is the devil offering Jesus? It isn't

really lordship over all the earth. That was to be the eternal Son of God's, by rightful inheritance from his Father. What the evil one dangles before the Son of Man is a *shortcut*, an easier path, to a goal that otherwise will require the ultimate sacrifice to reach. The devil is counting on hearing the cry of human suffering that says, "I'd do anything if this could just be over!" *Anything.* Satan, the "adversary" of both God and man, knows exactly what he is setting before Jesus—a way to bypass it all. Not only the hunger and weakness his frail flesh is suffering now in the desert, but all that it would suffer in the future. The wilderness is only the beginning, for Jesus knows where the next three years of his life are going . . . and he knows how the final three days of his life will end (Matt. 16:21).

So the tempter makes his pitch: "Might I offer you another option? A different colored robe? Maybe something . . . with less red in it?" Later, the devil will make this offer again, this time speaking through the loving, though misguided, heart of one of Jesus's own devoted followers: "God forbid it, Lord! This must never happen to you" (Matt. 16:22). And we know who Jesus rebuked when Peter uttered those words.

The heart of man is revealed in temptation.
Man knows his sin,
which without temptation he could never have known;
for in temptation, man knows on what he has set his heart.

Worship Me
Matthew 4:9

TODAY WE COME TO THE HEART OF IT. THE EVIL ONE'S most vile and ultimate goal is now obvious, making all else a prelude. By means of his opening temptations, the devil sought to get Jesus to do two things: to *distrust* the goodness of his Father and to *test* the Father's love for him. Two sides of the same coin—"*If you are the Son of God.*" But in this final temptation, the tempter goes further. In fact, he reaches (overreaches, as it happily turns out) for the grand prize: tempting Jesus to *abandon* his Father altogether, to withdraw the gift of a Son's love for his Father and give it to another. "Worship *me.*"

Lucifer (for now that he has shown his true colors, we may call him by that deceitful name he bears as "light-bringer" deformed into lord of all darkness)—Lucifer presents obeisance to himself as a small price to be paid for the great relief Jesus would enjoy. Jesus could be Lord without being Lamb. All he has to do is step over a thin line. Barely noticeable really. Like an invisible border between two countries. It would only take a moment. "Bow your head to me instead of bowing it under that cross. Fall down here on the mountaintop . . . or fall down in the dirty streets of Jerusalem."

This is the dark shadow that lies behind all of Lucifer's shimmering and fanciful temptations: to get us to switch sides, to change allegiances, to forget God. Then, in forgetting God, we would forget where we came from, where we are going, and where we belong—and welcome the numbing spiritual amnesia that wipes away our last faint memories of Paradise, taking with them those niggling longings for "home" that still trouble our souls. On the mountain with Jesus, this is precisely Lucifer's design because, in some cultures, if you can successfully convert the king, you will automatically get all the people with him. Turn the shepherd, and the sheep will naturally follow. In this case, of course, what didn't work with the shepherd might still work with the sheep.

[Lastly], Satan comes . . . in his wholly unconcealed display of
power as the prince of this world.
Now Satan fights with his very own weapons.
There is no more veiling, no more dissimulation.
His gift is immeasurably big and beautiful and alluring;
and in return for this gift he claims—worship.

It Is Written
Matthew 4:4

TODAY WE MAKE A TURN AND CHANGE THE ANGLE OF our view of temptation. To this point, we have been looking at the tempter's actions and listening to his words. Today we begin to look at Jesus's response and hear his words. We already know that, as deadly and cunning as the devil's tactics were, Jesus was able successfully to resist each one. Yes, as the Son of Man, Jesus was tempted in every respect as we are, but unlike us, he never succumbed to those temptations. He never sinned (Heb. 4:15). Having the nature of Adam and Eve, he could have made choices like Adam and Eve. But he did not. Instead, what did he do?

It is written, said Jesus, in response to each of the tempter's ploys. In every case, the living Word of God prevailed over his enemy by quoting the written Word of God. Jesus himself did what St. Paul would later exhort all of Christ's followers to do. To stand against the wiles of the devil, he wrote, we must put on the whole "armor of God," and then stand strong, prepared to wield "the sword of the Spirit, which is the word of God" (see Eph. 6:10–17). But let us take note here. Jesus did not speak the words of the Bible like some kind of incantation, as if by his merely pronouncing the sacred syllables correctly, the devil would be forced to flee. No. On the day of temptation, Jesus could brandish the Word *with* power and authority because, every day before that, he lived *by* that power and *under* that authority. His sharp weapon was also his daily bread.

95

Lead Us Not into Temptation

No wonder the first Scripture Jesus quoted, even as he hungered in the desert, declared that the Word of God was the source of his life and the true sustenance of his relationship with the Father. Quoting from the book of Deuteronomy (the source of all three of Jesus's quotations—something we will examine further tomorrow), Jesus recalled God's message to the people of Israel (see Deut. 8:1–3): "The manna that I provide every morning is more than food. It is a daily reminder that your lives are utterly dependent on me. This bread from heaven is a lifeline to earth. It keeps you always looking *to* me, staying *with* me, and living *by* me."

Unlike the Israelites—unlike us—Jesus had no other appetites to compete with his hunger for God. When he quoted these words, he meant them. They were his testimony (Rev. 12:11). So the tempter had to move on to try something else.

In his temptation, Jesus is robbed of all his own strength. . . .
He is left with nothing but the saving, supporting, enduring
Word of God, which holds him firmly and which fights
and conquers for him.

The Lord Your God
Matthew 4:7

THE BOOK OF DEUTERONOMY IS THE LAST OF THE FIVE
books of Moses known as the Torah, or the Pentateuch.
It is presented as a series of three long farewell speeches given
to the Israelites by Moses, just before he dies, and as the people
stand at the threshold of their entry into the Promised Land.
Moses reviews the lows and the highs in their forty-year journey
through the wilderness, recounting God's dramatic handiwork
on their behalf and re-presenting them with the divine laws
that were to direct their new life of liberation. Above all, Moses
dedicates his final words to making an impassioned call—
summoning Israel to a life of enduring loyalty to the Lord *their*
God. Three times Jesus quotes from Moses's speech as he does
battle with the tempter during his own sojourn in the wilderness.
Three times he answers his adversary's twisted lure of betrayal
with the language of Moses's call to fidelity.

"Do not put the LORD *your God* to the test" (Deut. 6:16). If
submissive obedience was all that God required of Israel, the
command "Do not put the LORD to the test" would have been
enough. The words "your God" could have been left out. But
read the larger context from which this verse comes (Deut.
6:4–16). The Lord did not deliver Israel from Egypt so that they
could trade in one oppressor for another. Servitude is *not* the
same as loyalty. The Lord was *their* God and they were *God's*
people. This is what the covenant meant to Moses on the hills

overlooking Canaan; it is what it meant to Jesus in the desert of Judea; and it is what it means to us in the wilderness of Lent. Putting the Lord to the test means putting unconditional love to the test. It's an oxymoron really. We do it—just as Israel did it at Massah when they forgot that the Lord was among them (Exod. 17:1–7)—but it really doesn't make much sense.

So, when Jesus quotes this verse to the devil, he is declaring with words what his life is already saying—the Lord is *his God*. Always has been, is now, and forever shall be! Every temptation, as difficult or unpleasant as it may be, is an occasion for us to choose the same. In temptation, *we* are the ones being put to the test. Whether we stand or fall (and we will surely do both!), we will always be God's people. But will the Lord always be *our God*?

> *Jesus' answer [to Satan] with the Word of God shows,*
> *first of all,*
> *that even the Son of God stands under the Word of God,*
> *and that he can and will claim no individual right*
> *beside this Word.*

The Adversary
Matthew 4:10

WE HAVE SEEN THAT, IN HIS FINAL TEMPTATION OF JESUS, the devil is entirely unmasked. Gone are all of his subtle tactics, his sneaky arguments and indirect questions. He attacks Jesus head-on, offering a straight-out trade: boundless glory for total betrayal. (Jesus most surely understood—painfully so— the deep turmoil suffered by Judas, who essentially was offered the same deal.)

But if the tempter is bold, Jesus is bolder. It's almost as if Jesus had had enough as he let loose his final words of opposition: "That's enough! It was necessary that I give you your chance, but you have failed. Away with you, Satan!" For the first time, Jesus addresses the devil using the name by which he is known in the Hebrew, the name that describes him to the core: *adversary*. Though the tempter did not present himself this way to Adam and Eve, there is no question that it was as "adversary" that he slithered into their world. He was offering the same deal to them too—*be like God by betraying God*. In fact, it is the only deal the adversary knows, and ever since Eden he has been offering it in an unlimited number of personally designed colors, shapes, and sizes. We can wonder if Jesus's anger at Satan when he drove him away was provoked in part by the recollection of what wreckage the adversary had left after he won his first round with humanity.

In fact, the adversary's conquest in the garden was precisely why Jesus was now fighting alone with him in the desert. There

99

in the wilderness, while suffering from loneliness and want, Jesus would begin to win back what we had lost in Paradise, while enjoying companionship and prosperity. No wonder Jesus quotes these particular words from Deuteronomy 6 about always sticking with God. Back then, Moses was worried that, once the people left the wilderness and began to know fruitful gardens once again, they too would forget their God and start following others (see Deut. 6:10–13). It turns out that Moses had good reason to worry. So Jesus quotes him. Jesus does what Adam and Eve failed to do, thus leaving us with the possibility of doing the same, when the adversary comes to offer his deal to us.

Either the Adam in me is tempted—in which case we fall.
Or the Christ in me is tempted—
in which case Satan is bound to fall.

Angels Came
Matthew 4:11

J ESUS MUST HAVE BEEN EXHAUSTED. HE HAD TO HAVE been
thoroughly worn out by this ordeal, this brutal struggle of
body, soul, and spirit—enduring his forty-day sojourn alone in
the wild, denying himself the comforts of earth, and renouncing
the temptations of hell. Finally, at the command of the Son of
God, the devil leaves the scene (more about this tomorrow),
and in his stead, angels from heaven come to "wait on" Jesus.
The Greek word for "wait on" used here by Matthew is the same
word from which we know the office of "deacon" (see Acts 6:1–
3)—those who wait on tables, who bring relief, who provide
the means of living. Yes, quite literally like table servers, angels
descended to Jesus in the valley of shadow, and there prepared a
table in the presence of his enemy (see Ps. 23:4–5).

Angels came, and in their coming all three of the adversary's
hellish temptations were converted into divine provisions. First,
Jesus denied himself the bread of trickery and received the bread
of kindness from the hands of angels. He whose only food was to
do the will of the Father (John 4:34) was fed by heavenly waiters.
Then, Jesus denied himself what he could have demanded by his
divine right as Son. He refused to coerce the Father into sending
angels to defend him. Now, angels are freely sent from God as
messengers (Gk. *angelos*) and bringers of love. Finally, Jesus
denied himself the easy road, the painless path. He who emptied
himself to take on our mortal nature (Phil. 2:6–7) refused to

reach up and grab divine glory for himself. In return, hands from heaven reached down and gently held his weakened body and soul until he healed. With what tenderness they carried out their mission of mercy.

When, by the help of God, we turn down the misleading enticements of the tempter, or resist the misdirected lusts of our own hearts, we find that God is there, ready to give better versions—*true* versions—of what we had denied ourselves. When Jesus gave himself over to his adversary's torments, were the angels watching the entire drama as it played out before the eyes of heaven? Were they impatient to rush to Jesus's side? Are they ready to rush to ours? The answer would be yes, for "are not all angels spirits in the divine service, sent to serve for the sake of those who are to inherit salvation?" (Heb. 1:14).

He who has entered into all weakness,
but who has been upheld by the Word,
receives from an angel of God refreshment of all his powers
of body, soul, and spirit.

The Devil Left . . . Until
Luke 4:13

BEFORE MOVING INTO HOLY WEEK AND THE FINAL DAYS
of these reflections on the "problem" of temptation, let's
stop for a moment to catch our breath. Since we began on Ash
Wednesday we've covered a lot of ground . . . and a lot of time!
From Adam and Eve in the Garden of Eden to Jesus in the
wilderness of Judea. Of course, that's the point of exploring this
subject during Lent. The life our parents lost in Paradise—a life
of unbroken companionship with God and with each other; a
life of boundless creativity and fruitfulness; a life that is "good"
in every conceivable way (Gen. 1:31)—that life would have been
gone forever had not the "new Adam" come to win it back for us.
And not without cost. An unimaginably heavy cost.

When he subjected himself to the devil's attacks, Jesus was
paying part of that cost. Remember, he was tempted like us in
every way, but without sin. In obedience to the Father, the Son
of Man gave our adversary another shot at ruining God's plans
for humanity, but this time things did not go so well for the
serpent. So he left . . . for the time being. "Until an opportune
time," says Luke.

As we learned yesterday, the pain of temptation is not
relentless. Thankfully, there comes a time when the devil does
leave and angels do come. And despite the ever-present trials
caused by our own distorted desires, even their stormy waves
sometimes subside. Still, the suffering of temptation is an

inherent piece of our human condition. If it were not, then the Son of God would have had no reason to submit himself to its violent blows. Today, as we are about to enter the most profound and mysterious week of the year, we are readying ourselves to celebrate the complete upending of the tempter's first designs. But not before the shadows return. Darkness waits for its opportunity to come back (Lk. 22:53).

> *By the temptation of Jesus Christ*
> *the temptation of Adam is brought to an end.*

HOLY
WEEK

God Oversees It All
Luke 22:31–34

TODAY WE ENTER HOLY WEEK, THE SACRED PATH LAID with the stones of Jesus's passion and death that leads directly to the gate of Easter. There, reminiscent of our ancestral home, we will enter a new garden (John 19:41), but not before passing through thorns and thistles such as the cursed ground has never brought forth before (Gen. 3:18). It is the kind of rocky path that makes fertile soil for the seeds of temptation. This is a week to pay attention and to be careful (Lk. 22:46). And if we are in some small measure confronted by the tempter's ruse, and especially if (when) we fall to it, we should not add to our failing the sin of despair. The testimony of one of God's own pillars, who tripped and fell headlong on this path, may give us pause.

Luke tells us that at the moment Peter made his third and final denial of Christ, the cock crowed, and as it did, Jesus turned to face Peter and looked him straight in the eye (Lk. 22:54–62). As if they were direct windows to his heart, Peter's eyes took in that look and then irresistibly shattered into tears of bitter shame. Peter broke ranks when his loyalty to Jesus was put to the test. "I don't know the man!"—the thing that Jesus predicted would happen and that Peter denied would happen . . . happened.

But Peter's fall to temptation tells us something—something we can be certain of beyond a shadow of a doubt. (For we also are among the brethren Peter will strengthen after he turns.)

Lead Us Not into Temptation

We learn from Jesus's admonition to Peter—"Simon, Simon, listen!"—that God is supervising the whole matter. God is neither shaken by its happening nor doubtful of its outcome. In his warning to Peter, Jesus makes it sound as if there had been some kind of behind-the-scenes negotiation going on between God and the devil. It wouldn't be the first such bargaining (Job 1:12; 2:6). Peter's darkest hour was at the same time a divinely "appointed" hour, and not a minute of it went by beyond the watchful gaze of heaven. So, when Jesus looked at his disciple, it was not to show Peter his sad disappointment but his unwavering love. All the while Jesus must have known that, because of the horrific and wonderful events that were about to take place, it wouldn't be long before Peter would have the chance to renew his oath of fidelity and once again return to the side of his Master (John 21:15–17).

*The Bible makes it clear that nothing can happen on earth
without the will and permission of God.
Satan is also in God's hands.
He must—against his will—serve God.
It is true that Satan has power,
but only where God "allows" it to him.*

Rocks and Obstacles
Matthew 18:7

S INCE WE BEGAN THESE REFLECTIONS, ALMOST SIX WEEKS
ago, the source of most all of the temptation we have
discussed has been found in a kind of toxic brew, a blend of
our own desires mixed with the work of our spiritual adversary.
There is another cause of temptation that we ignore to our
personal detriment and most definitely to the detriment of
others. It is the temptation that we sometimes cause, and
sometimes simply *are*, to one another. All we need to do is
revisit the story of Adam and Eve to find indisputable evidence
that our lives are interconnected in such an intimate way that
our sin—our personal falls to temptation—can have spiritual
consequences for others, especially those closest to us.

Jesus reserved some of his fiercest denouncement for
those who led others astray. Having seen, by now, that this is
the single most-focused aim of the devil—to put obstacles in
the way of God's children—we can understand the strength of
Jesus's language. The serpent is compelled by his agenda for
the ruin of humankind, and he is always recruiting others as
coconspirators. This is not a company with which we would like
to be associated. But we sometimes are (remember Peter). If we
pay close attention to the events that took place in Jerusalem
this week, we will surely find ourselves somewhere in the story.
There are many key players whose choices and actions were
driven by nefarious motivations. Others simply gave way to

that most human of impulses: self-survival. Yet they—*we*—all share equally in the burden of blame for the end result. Sin, in its many forms, begets death, in its many forms.

Of course, it is impossible to tell, much less to measure, all of the ways in which we cause others to stumble. Rarely do we set out to intentionally cause harm or scandal to our brother or sister, which means that most of the obstacles we put in one another's way are quite invisible to our own eyes. But what if we *could* see them? What if they appeared before us like so many rocks, not on our path, but on the path of the sister or brother walking next to us?

> *We should tell the devil that Jesus has called to himself*
> *not the righteous but sinners,*
> *and that we—in defiance of the devil—*
> *wish to remain sinners in order to be with Jesus,*
> *rather than be righteous with the devil.*

You Have Stood by Me
Luke 22:28

JESUS SPENT THE LAST NIGHT OF HIS LIFE IN THE COMPANY of his closest disciples, those who were his followers, whom he also called his friends (John 15:15). Relationships with Jesus that perhaps had started out of curiosity (John 1:38) and awe (Lk. 5:8) had grown into deep affection and loyalty. Even love. Which is what makes some of the events of that final night so extraordinarily painful, and the way Jesus describes his "friends" so amazingly curious. "You are those who have stood by me in my trials," he says to the Twelve. Once again, the word translated as "trials" could just as accurately be translated as "temptations." In Jesus's ongoing conflicts with the tempter—some witnessed by crowds in the streets, some witnessed only by heaven in the stillness of the night—he had known the growing friendship and faithfulness of a few chosen disciples whom he gratefully says stuck with him through it all.

But look at the verses that immediately precede Jesus's commendation. Even over their last supper together (according to John, it's likely that Jesus had just washed their feet!), the Twelve are disputing about which one of them is the greatest (Lk. 22:24–27). This is loyalty? This is standing by Jesus in his time of trial? And consider what is about to take place, despite Jesus's warning: "You will all become deserters because of me this night" (Matt. 26:31). This is friendship? This is faithfulness? Yet, sandwiched between these two acts of betrayal—proud ambition and selfish abandonment—Jesus calls these men steadfast. What does he see in them?

Jesus knew his disciples not for what they were that night, but for what he would make of them *because* of that night. James writes that steadfastness is actually the fruit of trial and temptation (Jas. 1:2–3). The ability to stand by Jesus—for that matter, the ability to stand by one another (Gal. 6:1–2)—is contingent upon our *learning* to be steadfast, a lesson that can only be taught in the school of temptation.

> *God gives opportunity to Satan*
> *in order to bring believers to salvation.*
> *Only by knowledge of sin,*
> *suffering and death can the new man live.*

Able to Help
Hebrews 2:17–18

JESUS COMMENDED THE DISCIPLES FOR THEIR STEADFASTNESS
in standing with him through his times of trial and
temptation (Lk. 22:28). Their companionship clearly meant a
great deal to him and, despite what we know of their frailty—
rather, *because* of what we know of it—we are moved by Jesus's
words of gratitude. But if we are to speak of real "stick-to-it-
iveness" through hell and high water—*our* hell and high water—
we are the ones who must be grateful. By becoming like us in
every respect, Jesus endured temptation in every respect. Will
he then abandon us in our wilderness or desert us when we
are in danger? Mercy and Faithfulness are Jesus's surnames,
inherited from his Father, and it is impossible for him to deny
himself. Therefore, it is we who can say with thankfulness, "You
are the One who has stood by me in my trials."

On the night of his betrayal, all twelve of Jesus's closest
followers fell down hard under the weight of their own personal
temptations. That night was, as Jesus said, in the hands of
darkness (Lk. 22:53), and each of his companions lost their way
in the shadows. We look at the events of those hours and we are
not surprised. It takes only a little self-knowledge to understand
that we would have done the same. Or worse. So we shouldn't
be surprised either that eleven of the twelve came through
those shadows stronger—more merciful and more faithful—for
having fallen. "He is able to help those who are being tested,"

113

says the writer to the Hebrews. Some of that help may surely come during the testing . . . but some of it cannot come until after.

St. Augustine wrote, "Our life as pilgrims cannot be free from temptation, for it is through temptation that we advance. None know themselves if they have not been tempted, nor can they be crowned unless they conquer, or conquer unless they struggle, or struggle unless they meet the enemy and be attacked." The bishop of Hippo and onetime recalcitrant knew of what he spoke. He, together with Jesus's first companions, tells us that Holy Week, while certainly a week for grief, is also a week for hope.

The temptation of Christ was harder, unspeakably harder,
than the temptation of Adam. . . .
Christ bore in himself the whole burden of the flesh,
under the curse,
under condemnation; and yet his temptation brought forth help
and salvation to all flesh.

Willing Spirit, Weak Flesh
Mark 14:38

THIS ABOUT SUMS IT UP. IN JUST A FEW WORDS, JESUS identifies the crux of our problem with temptation. He acknowledges rather generously that Peter, James, and John *want* to stay with him, to watch with him and pray with him, as he enters into the struggle of this terrible night. (Remember when the devil left him in the wilderness, "until an opportune time"? This night, in the Garden of Gethsemane, was surely one of those times.) But they seem unable to make the actions of their bodies conform to the affections of their hearts. Their weak flesh is stronger than their willing spirit.

What can they—we—do about it? Most of these reflections through Lent have been addressing the issue of temptation during or after the fact. By that I mean we have been looking at temptations as they have been happening—How can they be resisted? What happens when we fall? How do we recover? But there is also a *preventative* treatment for temptation, a medicine for the spirit that can help the flesh be awake and ready when the tempter comes knocking.

Remember what we have been saying from the start, that from our adversary's point of view, getting the flesh to do "bad" things is not the primary purpose of temptation. Moving the flesh in the wrong direction is simply a harmful means to a deadly end. The primary purpose is to get us to turn away from God—"to switch sides, to change our allegiances, to betray our loyalty." But what if we were turned toward him all the time? "Pray," said Jesus to his disciples. Jesus had come purposely to this garden to pray, and because of his prayer, he stayed faithful to the course that his Father had set before him (Mk. 14:36). "Pray." Put another way—talk with God. And keep on talking. And then talk some more. Prayer is the language of a relationship, not a religious practice. The more we grow to love God, the less inclined we will be to leave him. And we grow in love with him by being with him. "Pray." Jesus has accomplished in his flesh what is impossible for our flesh to accomplish without him. So staying *with Jesus* is the best antidote to temptation that there is. "Pray."

> *As in Adam's temptation all flesh fell,*
> *so in the temptation of Jesus Christ all flesh has been snatched*
> *away from the power of Satan.*

■ ■ ■

Our look at temptation ends here, where the Lenten journey has delivered us to the three great days of the Paschal Triduum. Jesus's prayer in the Garden of Gethsemane gives us the model by which we can all say to the Father, "Not my will but yours be done." By praying these words "in the flesh," Jesus makes it possible for us to do the same, and such a prayer always pulls the fangs right out of the serpent's lying mouth. Tomorrow, Good Friday, there will be no reflection, at least not on this subject. For Holy Saturday—a day of waiting . . . and praying—we offer a few concluding thoughts. Then, for Easter—well, that'll be a good day to stop reflecting, or thinking . . . and start singing.

A Reading from Psalm 22

My God, my God, why have you forsaken me?
Why are you so far from helping me, from the words of my
  groaning?
O my God, I cry by day, but you do not answer;
and by night, but find no rest.

Yet you are holy,
enthroned on the praises of Israel.
In you our ancestors trusted;
they trusted, and you delivered them.
To you they cried, and were saved;
in you they trusted, and were not put to shame.

But I am a worm, and not human;
scorned by others, and despised by the people.
All who see me mock at me;
they make mouths at me, they shake their heads;
"Commit your cause to the LORD; let him deliver—
let him rescue the one in whom he delights!"

Yet it was you who took me from the womb;
you kept me safe on my mother's breast.
On you I was cast from my birth,
and since my mother bore me you have been my God.
Do not be far from me,
for trouble is near

and there is no one to help.
I am poured out like water,
and all my bones are out of joint;
my heart is like wax;
it is melted within my breast;
my mouth is dried up like a potsherd,
and my tongue sticks to my jaws;
you lay me in the dust of death.

I will tell of your name to my brothers and sisters;
in the midst of the congregation I will praise you:
You who fear the LORD, praise him!
All you offspring of Jacob, glorify him;
stand in awe of him, all you offspring of Israel!
For he did not despise or abhor
the affliction of the afflicted;
he did not hide his face from me,
but heard when I cried to him.

To him, indeed, shall all who sleep in the earth bow down;
before him shall bow all who go down to the dust,
and I shall live for him.
Posterity will serve him;
future generations will be told about the Lord,
and proclaim his deliverance to a people yet unborn,
saying that he has done it.

Verses 1–11, 14–15, 22–24, 29–31 (NRSV)

From Garden to Desert to Garden

> *For the LORD will comfort Zion;*
> *he will comfort all her waste places,*
> *and will make her wilderness like Eden,*
> *her desert like the garden of the Lord;*
> *joy and gladness will be found in her,*
> *thanksgiving and the voice of song.*
> *Isaiah 51:3*

GOD PLANTED A GARDEN TO BE THE HOME FOR OUR FIRST parents. A garden for them to till, to keep, and to enjoy. Eden was to be the ground where heaven and earth would convene—a garden to be a meeting place for God and the children born of his love, where they could walk together "in the cool of the day" and enjoy the fruits of their labors.

From the moment the serpent first caught Eve's attention, a third party inserted itself into this liaison. The tempter interjected another possible relationship for Adam and Eve, a different voice to listen to, a different option to follow. We struck up a new alliance, thinking that it would not cost us the old one. The consequences, as we have seen, would be disastrous for all of us. We know that part of the sad result of our ancestors' "fall to temptation" would be the "thorns and thistles" that, thenceforth, would symbolize the earth's broken state. As hard as he would work, Adam would never be able to reproduce the flowers and fruits of Paradise. Even more difficult—impossible, really—would be cultivating the relationship of love that he once shared with his Maker. If that were to be mended and brought back to life, it would have to be done by the Gardener himself.

When Jesus followed the leading of the Spirit into the desert—into the arms of his adversary and ours—he went with the purpose of reclaiming the fallen wasteland and wresting the children of Adam and Eve from the serpent's deadly grip. Actually, from the moment of Mary's *Fiat*, the wilderness began its gentle repair, but, here in the deserts of Judea, God's Hoe would make a forceful swing at the hard ground. For three years that swinging went on relentlessly, and with each wounding blow, a softer earth brought forth new sprouts of heaven. Waste places were being reborn. The hope of Eden—the *possibility* of Eden—was being reimagined.

But, though he was losing ground day after day, the "ancient foe" still did not give up. Finally, the "opportune time" he was waiting for came one dark night outside Jerusalem. *Gethsemane* means "oil press," and within its garden walls the serpent started to squeeze the life out of the Son of Man. Less than a day would pass before God's chosen Tool for recultivating the earth would be broken in pieces atop the waste place of Golgotha. The desert land's foul keeper rested easy that night, believing that was the end of spring . . . forever.

But another garden—an ever-so-small one—became the planting ground for the fallen Seed of Golgotha. In the silence of that same night, and through the stillness of the Sabbath day, something stirred deep within its soil. In those shrouded hours, the Son of God dug so deeply into the fallen world that he reached the holding place of Adam and Eve's banishment, and there, before the astonished and terrified eyes of their keeper, he pulled them up by their roots and took them in his outstretched arms. Leaving the serpent to writhe in his fury, the King of glory reopened the gates and replanted his children in Paradise, where they belonged.

From there, from the cursed ground's embrace, heaven's Seed sprung up like a youthful shoot. The Tree of Life—from which we forever had been expelled—instead came forth to us. From a tomb its trunk stretched to the sky, once again rejoining earth to heaven. And from its sacred branches new fruit hung, sweet, delicious, and free to take and eat.

> *O happy fault, O necessary sin of Adam,*
> *which gained for us so great a Redeemer!*
> *The power of this holy night dispels all evil,*
> *washes guilt away, restores lost innocence,*
> *brings mourners joy;*
> *it casts out hatred, brings us peace,*
> *and humbles earthly pride.*
> *Night truly blessed, when heaven is wedded to earth*
> *and man is reconciled with God!*

Exultet (sixth century)

Notes

Quotations from Dietrich Bonhoeffer, *"Creation and Fall" and "Temptation,"* trans. John C. Fletcher and Kathleen Downham (New York: Simon & Schuster / Touchstone, 1997) are as follows. Used by permission.

On page 16:
   "The temptation of the devil drives the Christian afresh into the arms of Jesus Christ, the Crucified." From page 137.

On page 18:
   "The place in which all temptation originates is my evil desires. My own longing for pleasure, and my fear of suffering, entice me to let go of the Word of God." From page 126.

On page 20:
   "Temptation is a power which is stronger than any creature. It is the invasion of Satan's power into the world of creation." From page 124.

On page 22:
   "Temptation is seduction, leading astray. Therefore it is of the devil, for the devil is a liar." From page 124.

On page 26:
   "Unforgiven, cherished sin is the best gateway by which the devil can invade our hearts." From page 141.

On page 28:
   "The Christian recognizes the cunning of Satan. Suddenly, doubt has been sowed in his heart, suddenly everything is uncertain." From page 113.

On page 30:
   "The God who causes day and night to be also gives seasons of thirst and seasons of refreshment; he gives storms and peace, times of grief and fear, and times of joy." From page 113.

On page 32:
   "God shows himself in temptation not as the gracious, the near one, who furnishes us with all the gifts of the Spirit; on the contrary, it is as if he forsakes us, he is quite distant from us; we are in the wilderness." From page 118.

On page 34:
   "The lust of the flesh is nothing other than the anguish of the flesh in the face of death." From page 133.

On page 36:
   "[Satan] plans to make the flesh rebellious towards the spirit. Satan knows that the flesh is afraid of suffering." From page 119.

On page 38:

"We have all had the dream that we desire to flee from something horrible and cannot. This is the ever-recurring knowledge in our subconscious of the true situation of fallen man." From page 91.

On page 42:

"The tempter is only to be found where there is innocence. . . where there is guilt, he has already gained power." From page 116.

On page 44:

"The voice of the tempter does not come out of an abyss only recognized as 'Hell.' It completely conceals its origin. . . . The denial of the origin belongs to the essence of the seducer." From page 116.

On page 46:

"We should never argue with the devil about our sins, but we should speak about our sins only with Jesus." From page 141.

On page 48:

"'Has God really said?' In the abyss of this question, Adam sinks, and with him the whole of mankind." From page 117.

On page 50:

"Let us be on our guard against such cunning exaggerations of God's command. The evil one is certainly in them." From page 75.

On page 52:

"Thus the conversation goes on—the first conversation about God. . . . It is not prayer, or calling upon God together, but speaking about God, going beyond him." From page 76.

On page 54:

"Satan does not fill us with hatred of God, but with forgetfulness of God." From page 132.

On page 58:

"Adam is no longer creature. He has torn himself away from his creature-liness. [He] no longer needs the Creator, he has become a creator himself." From page 80.

On page 60:

"The word 'disobedience' does not exhaust the facts of this case. It is revolt. . . . It is defection. The Fall affects the whole of the created world which is henceforth plundered." From page 84.

On page 62:

"Man's shame is his reluctant acknowledgement . . . of God. [Shame] must give witness to its own fallen state." From page 88.

On page 64:

"Man has suddenly fallen from God and is still in flight. The Fall is not enough for him; he cannot flee fast enough." From page 90.

On page 66:

"Instead of surrendering, Adam falls back on one art learned from the serpent, that of correcting God." From page 92.

Notes

On page 68:

"With curse and promise God speaks to fallen, unreconciled, fleeing Adam. Adam is preserved alive in a world between curse and promise, and the last promise is the permission to die. Paradise is destroyed." From page 93.

On page 70:

"From the time of Adam's expulsion from paradise, every man is born with this question, which Satan has put in Adam's heart. That is the first question of all flesh: 'Has God really said?'" From page 117.

On page 74:

"The temptation which led to man's fall and the temptation which led to Satan's fall—all other temptations in human history have to do with these two stories of temptation. Either we are tempted in Adam or we are tempted in Christ." From page 115.

On page 76:

"'Lead us not into temptation.' He who taught the disciples to pray in this way was Jesus Christ, who alone must have known what temptation was." From page 115.

On page 78:

"If Jesus was to help man, who is flesh, he had to take upon himself the whole temptation experience of the flesh. Even Jesus Christ was born [in the flesh] with the question: 'Has God really said?'—yet without sin." From page 117.

On page 80:

"Jesus is tempted in his flesh, in his faith, and in his allegiance to God. All three are the one temptation—to separate Jesus from the Word of God." From page 120.

On page 83:

"Satan tempts Jesus in the weakness of human flesh. . . . He wishes to set his Godhead against his manhood." From page 119.

On page 86:

"[Satan] piles on his temptation by himself quoting God's Word against Jesus. Even Satan can use God's Word in the struggle." From page 119.

On page 88:

"There is only one stronger reality to be set against the exclusive reality of desire and of Satan: the image and the presence of the Crucified." From page 132.

On page 92:

"The heart of man is revealed in temptation. Man knows his sin, which without temptation he could never have known; for in temptation, man knows on what he has set his heart." From page 128.

On page 94:

"[Lastly], Satan comes . . . in his wholly unconcealed display of power as the prince of this world. Now Satan fights with his very own weapons. There is no more veiling, no more dissimulation. His gift is immeasurably big and beautiful and alluring; and in return for this gift he claims—worship." From page 120.

Lead Us Not into Temptation

On page 96:
"In the temptation Jesus is robbed of all his own strength. . . . He is left with nothing but the saving, supporting, enduring Word of God, which holds him firmly and which fights and conquers for him." From page 121.

On page 98:
"Jesus' answer [to Satan] with the Word of God shows, first of all, that even the Son of God stands under the Word of God, and that he can and will claim no individual right beside this Word." From page 119.

On page 100:
"Either the Adam in me is tempted—in which case we fall. Or the Christ in me is tempted—in which case Satan is bound to fall." From page 115.

On page 102:
"He who has entered into all weakness, but who has been upheld by the Word, receives from an angel of God refreshment of all his powers of body, soul, and spirit." From page 121.

On page 104:
"By the temptation of Jesus Christ the temptation of Adam is brought to an end." From page 122.

On page 108:
"The Bible makes it clear that nothing can happen on earth without the will and permission of God. Satan is also in God's hands. He must—against his will—serve God. It is true that Satan has power, but only where God "allows" it to him." From page 127.

On page 110:
"We should tell the devil that Jesus has called to himself not the righteous but sinners, and that we—in defiance of the devil—wish to remain sinners in order to be with Jesus, rather than be righteous with the devil." From page 141.

On page 112:
"God gives opportunity to Satan in order to bring believers to salvation. Only by knowledge of sin, by suffering and death can the new man live." From page 129.

On page 114:
"The temptation of Christ was harder, unspeakably harder, than the temptation of Adam. . . .Christ bore in himself the whole burden of the flesh, under the curse, under condemnation; and yet his temptation brought forth help and salvation to all flesh." From page 117.

On page 116:
"As in Adam's temptation all flesh fell, so in the temptation of Jesus Christ all flesh has been snatched away from the power of Satan." From page 122.

About Paraclete Press
Who We Are

As the publishing arm of the Community of Jesus, Paraclete Press presents a full expression of Christian belief and practice—from Catholic to Evangelical, from Protestant to Orthodox, reflecting the ecumenical charism of the Community and its dedication to sacred music, the fine arts, and the written word. We publish books, recordings, sheet music, and video/DVDs that nourish the vibrant life of the church and its people.

What We Are Doing

BOOKS | PARACLETE PRESS BOOKS show the richness and depth of what it means to be Christian. While Benedictine spirituality is at the heart of who we are and all that we do, our books reflect the Christian experience across many cultures, time periods, and houses of worship.

We have many series, including *Paraclete Essentials*; *Paraclete Fiction*; *Paraclete Poetry*; *Paraclete Giants*; and for children and adults, *All God's Creatures*, books about animals and faith; and *San Damiano Books*, focusing on Franciscan spirituality. Others include *Voices from the Monastery* (men and women monastics writing about living a spiritual life today), *Active Prayer*, and new for young readers: *The Pope's Cat*. We also specialize in gift books for children on the occasions of Baptism and First Communion, as well as other important times in a child's life, and books that bring creativity and liveliness to any adult spiritual life.

THE MOUNT TABOR BOOKS series focuses on the arts and literature as well as liturgical worship and spirituality; it was created in conjunction with the Mount Tabor Ecumenical Centre for Art and Spirituality in Barga, Italy.

MUSIC | THE PARACLETE RECORDINGS label represents the internationally acclaimed choir *Gloriæ Dei Cantores*, the *Gloriæ Dei Cantores Schola*, and the other instrumental artists of the *Arts Empowering Life Foundation*.

Paraclete Press is the exclusive North American distributor for the Gregorian chant recordings from St. Peter's Abbey in Solesmes, France. Paraclete also carries all of the Solesmes chant publications for Mass and the Divine Office, as well as their academic research publications.

In addition, PARACLETE PRESS SHEET MUSIC publishes the work of today's finest composers of sacred choral music, annually reviewing over 1,000 works and releasing between 40 and 60 works for both choir and organ.

VIDEO | Our video/DVDs offer spiritual help, healing, and biblical guidance for a broad range of life issues including grief and loss, marriage, forgiveness, facing death, understanding suicide, bullying, addictions, Alzheimer's, and Christian formation.

Learn more about us at our website
www.paracletepress.com
or phone us toll-free at 1.800.451.5006

SCAN
TO
READ
MORE